"But I'm Almost 13!"

An Action Plan for Raising a Responsible Adolescent

KENNETH R. GINSBURG, M.D., M.S.Ed.
with **MARTHA M. JABLOW**

Contemporary Books

Chicago New York San Francisco Lisbon London Madrid Mexico City
Milan New Delhi San Juan Seoul Singapore Sydney Toronto

Library of Congress Cataloging-in-Publication Data

Ginsburg, Kenneth.
    "But I'm almost 13!" : an action plan for raising a responsible adolescent /
Kenneth Ginsburg and Martha Jablow.
       p.   cm.
    Includes bibliographical references and index.
    ISBN 0-8092-9717-5
       1. Parent and teenager—United States.   2. Teenagers—United States.
3. Adolescent psychology—United States.   4. Parenting—United States.
I. Jablow, Martha.   II. Title.

HQ799.15 .G56   2001
306.874—dc21   00-52384

Contemporary Books

A Division of The **McGraw-Hill** Companies

1 2 3 4 5 6 7 8 9 0   AGM/AGM   0 9 8 7 6 5 4 3 2 1

ISBN 0-8092-9717-5

This book was set in Adobe Garamond
Printed and bound by Quebecor Martinsburg

Cover design by Jennifer Locke
Cover photograph copyright © Elyse Lewin/Image Bank
Interior design by Jeanette Wojtyla

McGraw-Hill books are available at special quantity discounts to use as premiums and
sales promotions, or for use in corporate training programs. For more information, please
write to the Director of Special Sales, Professional Publishing, McGraw-Hill, Two Penn
Plaza, New York, NY 10121-2298. Or contact your local bookstore.

This book is printed on acid-free paper.

Contents

Acknowledgments

I dedicate this book to those who have taught me about the importance of adults in the lives of young people. To my grandmother, Belle Moore, who was as good a human being as is put on this earth. To my parents, Marilyn and Arnold, who modeled many of the finest parenting skills presented here. To my wife, Celia, who is as committed to raising kind, creative, responsible children as anyone I could imagine. To Ilana and Talia, who I expect will grow up to be wonderful people, who are the joys of my life, and who—in not so many years and in a fit of adolescent moodiness—will wave this book in front of my face and say, "And you thought you knew about kids?!"

I also acknowledge and thank several other important people: my professional mentors, Gail Slap and Don Schwarz, for modeling that caring is central to the practice of medicine; Jacqui, who has demonstrated how a committed parent can get her children through anything; and the thousands of young people and families who have let me into their lives to serve them as best I can.

—K. R. G.

If I had been blessed to know Ken Ginsburg and work on this book with him more than a decade ago, my teenagers would have been spared my many shortcomings. But we have survived adolescence! My daughter Cara is 26 and my son David is 24. They are wonderful, unique young adults. Their journeys through adolescence were occasionally challenging, often filled with good humor, and ultimately successful. I love them dearly for who they are and for all they have taught me.

I also wish to acknowledge Dr. Gail Slap, with whom I had the privilege of working on *Teenage Health Care*. Like Ken, she is a leader in adolescent medicine and an exceptional human being. Thank you, Gail, for suggesting to Ken that he ask me to collaborate on this book. Ken and I also thank our editor, Judith McCarthy, whose interest and support have been steadfast, and our agent, Philippa Brophy of Sterling Lord Literistic, for bringing us to Contemporary Books.

—M. M. J.

Introduction

As a pediatrician who specializes in adolescent medicine, my job is to keep young people safe, healthy, and alive. Preteens and teenagers come to see me for routine checkups or physical problems. I treat their asthma and acne and sprained ankles. I make sure that their immunizations are up-to-date. I talk with them about the many changes that their bodies are going through during puberty. But the most important part of my job does not involve their physical health. Instead, it focuses on guiding them toward positive behaviors.

The overwhelming majority of adolescent health problems result from behaviors—especially those involving alcohol, drugs, unsafe sex, reckless driving, and violence—or emotional problems such as sadness, anxiety, and depression. The startling reality is that 80 percent of teenage deaths result from automobile crashes (most often when alcohol and drugs are present), homicide, and suicide. All of those tragedies are preventable. Many physical problems, such as disordered eating, unplanned pregnancy, and sexually transmitted diseases, also result from adolescent behaviors.

To understand where I am coming from, you need to consider that for most of my career I have taken care of people after the fact—after they have become hurt or ill. I cannot tell you how frustrating and saddening it is to take care of young people who are harmed by tragedies that never should have happened. For that reason, my adolescent medicine colleagues and I put the *prevention of risk* at the top of our agenda.

The Question Is How to Prevent Risk

If only it were so simple as recognizing and telling young people to change their worrisome behaviors!

Looking for risk in teenagers is easy. When most people think of adolescents, the word *risk* flashes like a neon sign as if it is part of the basic definition of *teenager*. Yet my research and clinical practice have allowed me to listen to the perspectives of thousands of youths. This has enabled me to see them differently and more fully. I see their strengths, their optimism, their creativity, their resiliency. They have made me a strong believer that we adults must build upon those strengths if we are to prevent risk. As a parent, you are in an ideal position to do this.

Young people need much more than information to guide their behaviors. They need adults who understand and pay attention to how kids think and behave, who support them through emotional crises, and who know how to guide them toward safer, appropriate choices.

I have become so convinced of the power of adults in adolescents' lives that I have been training professional audiences for the past decade in how to assess youths before crises strike and move them away from destructive behaviors and toward more positive futures. But none of us professionals can be successful alone or all of the time. We know this essential truth: *Caring, proactive parents can do more than any of us possibly can—because parents are the most important people in their children's lives.*

Because I believe so deeply in parents' vital role, much of my energy now focuses on preparing parents to give the loving guidance that all children need, whether they ask for it or not. Yes, even when they ignore you, argue, or rebel against you, they want and need your attention. You are still the most powerful, influential person in their lives.

A strong, loving connection between your child and you may be the most protective factor in your child's life. Research backs me up on that fact, so stay focused on your child during these crucial years before adolescence.

Natural Concerns and the Good News

I imagine that you are anxious about your child's approaching adolescence—otherwise this book would not be in your hands. It is perfectly normal to worry about how both you and your child will manage and survive the next several years. I understand your concern. I see and hear it almost every day. When young people come to see me, they are usually accompanied by a parent, grandparent, or other adult relative. Some of these adults openly discuss their anxiety about adolescence. Others show it simply in their worried facial expressions or voices.

Our natural concern about how a child will weather adolescence is heightened by events close to home, like the metal detectors installed in the local school, and almost daily in newspapers and on television and radio. Adolescence is depicted widely as "turbulent" or the years of "storm and stress." [The common negative stereotype even crept into a crossword puzzle in *The New York Times* (April 24, 2000). The clue was "In the difficult years." The answer, of course, was "teenage."]

Movies, music, and magazines add to the hype that most teenagers are sex-obsessed, drug-using airheads with pierced, tattooed bodies or antisocial loners. No wonder adults expect the teen years to be tumultuous, dangerous, rebellious, downright scary for parents and kids alike.

Parents voice these universal concerns in my office and when I speak to groups around the country. They *fear* for their children's safety and survival between the presumed innocence of childhood and the independence of adulthood. Preteens themselves are less likely to confess their apprehension about adolescence. Some are brash and hide their fears with an "I'm tough" attitude. Others are quiet and withdrawn. Yet today's young people know enough about the world around them— even as early as age eight or nine—to worry about navigating adolescent storms.

The good news is usually overlooked: most children come through adolescence just fine—in sound physical and mental health. They have enormous talents, abilities, and resilience. Adolescence can be a great, positive experience for kids and their families. But that does not happen in a vacuum. It is not sheer luck. It occurs when parents and other adults in a child's life provide these vital ingredients:

love
trust
support
involvement
active guidance
gradually increasing freedom and responsibility

Always Keep the Door Open

My most rewarding work as a doctor is in creating a place where young people can talk safely about those parts of their lives that are producing stress. Whenever preteens or teenagers come to my office, I try to create a zone of safety for them. I want them to know that they can always come in and talk to me if they get into trouble. I want them to feel that they will never make a mistake by coming to see me. There is no penalty or punishment for seeking help. I am always there, if just to listen. I want parents to be able to do the same thing—to learn how to keep the doors open so that children will never feel they have made a mistake by going to their parents for help or guidance.

Prepare Now

Let's begin with a key point: do not wait until your child is fifteen or sixteen to think about how you will handle adolescent challenges. Several reasons for this will be discussed in greater detail later, but for the moment, trust me because this fact is absolutely essential: your child is more open to listening to you *now*, more likely to absorb your messages and values *now*, more interested in what you think *right now* between age nine and the early teens than he or she will be in mid- to late adolescence.

Preteens still want very much to please their parents. They will rarely tell you that, but they are not yet ready to throw out your ideas and standards. More outright challenge is still to come. During these preteen years, you have a golden opportunity to capitalize on their affection and desire to please you, so play it for all it's worth. You are in the driver's seat (perhaps quite

literally and too often), so you can use your position to guide
and to teach because they are watching you and listening closely.

Before they can challenge parents and move toward adult
independence, young teens must have a solid foundation—a
strong springboard from which to leap. You have been building
that launching pad from the day they were born. You have loved
them, cared for their physical and emotional needs, educated
them from infancy through childhood. In the critical period of
pre- and early adolescence, you must pay special attention to
preparing them for the future.

We cannot let them simply drift through their teenage
years. Children this age simply do not yet have the intellectual
capacity or the life experience to make mature decisions on their
own. They need us—parents, health care professionals, teachers, and other caring adults—to give them a steady hand and a
guiding compass.

During these transition years, young people wrestle with a
variety of new stresses. When they are under these pressures,
they will struggle for effective ways to cope. Some of their
choices will be productive and creative and will lead to responsible behaviors. Other choices could lead in the opposite direction, toward harmful or destructive behaviors. We cannot afford
to let them choose dangerous coping strategies. With our guidance, we can prepare them to deal creatively and positively with
their lives' challenges.

As we begin to discuss active ways of preparing children for
adolescence, I would like to give you a brief list of basics to keep
in mind:

• Play an active role in your child's life. Don't withdraw,
recede, or presume that your preteen does not need you as

much as he or she did a few years ago. Yes, kids this age can do much more for themselves—we have moved far beyond tying their shoelaces and selecting their clothes for them. They will even graciously point out to you how little they need or want you. They'll roll their eyes at your advice and inform you, "I'm almost 13!" implying how full of wisdom they already are. But they need parents as much as ever in their lives. Do not cut them loose to "learn from their mistakes." They simply are not ready.

• Don't throw up your hands and say, "This will pass. It's just a stage." Many of their roller-coaster emotions and behaviors are developmentally normal, and you should not have to jump into every problem. But pay close attention to their outbursts or quirky behaviors; watch and listen with your head and your heart.

• Don't cede your influence and involvement to their peers in the belief that children this age need or care for friends more than parents. Friends are certainly important and influential, but this does not make parents any less so.

• Don't buy into the belief that adolescents think they are invulnerable. You have probably heard statements like this: "Teenagers take risks because they think nothing bad will happen to them." That is actually untrue. They may *behave* recklessly, but most young people are really afraid of many of the same things we fear for them. They know the dangers, but they usually do not link present actions with future consequences (which we will discuss in Chapter 2), or they make serious mistakes while believing they actually enhance their safety. In other words, their actions do not always accurately reflect either their emotions or their thinking.

Preparing Through Skill-Building

"But I'm Almost 13!" offers specific skills and strategies to strengthen your relationship with your children and help them practice—in a safe, comfortable family environment—techniques that they can rely on when faced with peer pressure and risk behaviors that will surely come their way. If both you and your child are equipped with specific skills, your mutual preparation will translate into prevention of those adolescent problems that give parents nightmares.

Think of this process as any new skill you would teach a child—say, basketball. You demonstrate passing, and then you and your child practice passing back and forth as you both run down the court. You demonstrate shooting, and your child practices alongside you. The more practice, the stronger and more confident your child becomes. And the more any skill or strategy is practiced, the more easily it will come to a child when needed in a crunch.

If you were teaching your child to play basketball for the first time, you would not simply go to a court, shoot one layup, walk off the court, and expect your child to play like a pro. Or when teaching a young child to ride a bicycle, you would not give her a two-wheeler and say, "Just pedal." More than likely, you would jog alongside and hold onto the back of the seat to help maintain her balance until she got the hang of it.

My point is simply this: youths need teaching, demonstration, practice, ongoing support, encouragement, and reinforcement to master any physical skill. The same is true of social skills, such as learning how to resist peer pressure; to turn down cigarettes, drugs, liquor, and sex; or to negotiate their way safely out of dangerous situations—all without losing face or being ostracized as a wimp, loser, geek, or whatever word is in fashion the week you are reading this book. Social skills must be taught, practiced, reinforced, and repeated until they come as naturally to a kid as shooting a basket or riding a bike.

Today's Higher Costs

We adults need to be better prepared than ever before because today's young people face far more serious consequences than our generation did. When we were kids, getting into a fight meant a black eye or broken nose. Today it can result in a stab wound, gunshot, or death. When we were teenagers, the greatest concern about sex was unwanted pregnancy. Now unprotected sex can lead to long-term sexually transmitted diseases and/or death through HIV and AIDS. With these much higher stakes, young people are much more vulnerable. We must build in stronger protections.

Today, we simply cannot afford to let adolescents learn by their own mistakes. We must teach them the necessary skills and practice those skills with them. To return to the basketball analogy for a moment, we must help them practice for the big tournament, the Final Four years of high school.

What to Expect from This Book

Scare tactics are not my thing. I will not frighten you with a laundry list of risks to anticipate as your children move through adolescence. Instead, *"But I'm Almost 13!"* presents a series of strategies to help you fill the essential parental role of guiding your children and assuring their safety by building on their strengths.

Some parents want a book to provide a script for discussing sex, drugs, or violence with their children. I know that these subjects raise parents' anxiety levels, but this book is not intended to give you content—no magic words to explain sex or drugs. My goal is to help you develop your own style for guiding, disciplining, and improving your relationship with your children.

Do not expect dogma or theory on these pages. I do not prescribe any value system or ready-made formula for raising teenagers. Instead, I will offer you a framework to which you can attach your own values, beliefs, and standards. I will give you the information, techniques, and exercises to build a stronger relationship with your children, but you will adapt them to your own family.

You will find numerous anecdotes on these pages to illustrate the techniques that I am suggesting. While these examples are drawn from real life, they have been altered to protect individuals' privacy and assure confidentiality.

As you begin to read this book, you should also know that I have structured it much like my workshop presentations. It is designed to be a skills-building book—not a one-night read to breeze through and put on the shelf. This book is built upon process. If you are to get the most out of this book, you will go through it strategy by strategy, chapter by chapter, and stop to practice the skills presented.

To summarize the content and direction of *"But I'm Almost 13!,"* here is a preview: We will begin by looking back at your own adolescence in Chapter 1 because it is important to consider how you were parented and how that has influenced your own parenting style. Then we will examine how young people think (Chapter 2) and why that is critical to understanding their behaviors. A brief Chapter 3 will lay the foundation for a step-by-step approach to effecting behavioral change—to help you promote your child's constructive behaviors and prevent negative ones. The remaining chapters will elaborate on the steps described in Chapter 3. You will learn ways to make kids aware of problems and consider the consequences; to motivate kids to change behaviors and cope with peer pressure and stress; and to reinforce their positive behaviors by building a stronger environment of peers, older teens, and other adults. We also will discuss the futility of traditional lecturing and a more effective discipline approach—guiding, not punishing. We will discover ways to increase your child's independence safely. And we will learn how strengthening the parent-child connection through positive attention can diminish the need to discipline in the classic sense.

A Personal Postscript

I care passionately about young people. In fifteen years as a physician, I've treated thousands of amazing kids. I am also a parent. My wonderful twin daughters will become teenagers sooner than I can imagine. (Freezing them has not worked.) I hope you are picking up this book while your child is still a pre-teen, but if your son or daughter is already a teenager, remember that it is never too late to put these skills into practice.

1

Preparing Yourself for Your Child's Adolescence

"When I was your age . . ." Your kids roll their eyes when you begin a sentence with that phrase, right? They cannot imagine that we adults were ever young. Or if they do, they picture us in a black-and-white episode of "Leave It to Beaver" or as Technicolor tie-dyed hippies. Then they settle in for a long, boooor-rrrrring lecture on the good old days.

Parents and teens both assume that there is a huge gap between generations. Culturally, socially, technologically, that is true. We did not have E-mail and instant-messaging to contact our friends. We had to talk to them on the only telephone in the house. Most families did not have several extensions, different lines, and certainly no cell phones—so our parents were always hassling us, "Wind up that call. Hang up right now. I need the phone, and you need to do your homework."

When we were teenagers, we did not worry about whether our classmates carried guns into school. Marijuana was less potent then. If we had sex, we worried about pregnancy, but most of us did not even know about sexually transmitted diseases like chlamydia or human papilloma virus (HPV). Deadly HIV and AIDS had not arrived.

Yes, dramatic differences do exist between today's teens and their parents' adolescence, but there are many similarities as well. Developmentally, teenagers then and now move along the same emotional, psychological, social, and intellectual paths. The culture and environment have changed, but teenagers are teenagers in any decade. We parents need to recall our own adolescence—how we felt, what we thought, feared, hoped for. My point here—and I am deliberately beginning with this point—is that remembering and understanding how you felt, thought, and reacted and what you worried about when you were a teenager is essential if you are to guide your own children safely and successfully through adolescence.

Remember How You Were Parented

A good way to start this process is to reflect on your own adolescence. This is not a sentimental trip down memory lane. It is a way to remind you that you are entering the "parent of a teenager" phase with considerable preparation and expertise. You may not think you are ready, but you have a wealth of experience. You were an adolescent, too, and not that long ago. Reflecting on your own youthful experiences can help you understand and plan for your new role as the parent of an emerging teenager.

A Mind Game

Flip back a few decades and recall your relationship with your parents. Now consider these questions.

- What did you *like*—even then—about your relationship with them?

- What did they do well?

- What do you appreciate now, as an adult, about the ways they handled discipline and communication?

- What did you *dislike* about your relationship with your parents when you were a teenager?

- Why did you dislike or resent those aspects? Do you still dislike those things?

- How would you describe your parents' style? Rigid? Authoritarian? Dogmatic? Easygoing? Inconsistent? Distant? Try to recall specific examples of things they said or did to bring you to these conclusions.

- Did your parents jump in with criticism or advice before you had a chance to finish expressing your thoughts?

- Did they deny or denigrate your emotions with comments like "You shouldn't feel that way . . . It's not that bad . . . Don't be foolish . . ." or "You can't possibly hate your brother."

- If you grew up in a two-parent household, was one parent strict or aloof while the other was warmer, more nurturing and accepting? Did they stand together and back each other up like Carol and Mike Brady—and even Alice? Or could you play one against the other to get your way? Did they waffle when it came to setting limits so that you never knew whether your behavior would spark a scream or a shrug?

Take some time to answer these questions thoughtfully. They are not idle or theoretical questions. Let them rumble around in your head for a day or two before you try to answer them. You may want to discuss them with your brothers and sisters. Or get in touch with an old friend or two from that period in your life. Rehash some of the experiences you shared in middle school or junior high. Dust off an old school yearbook or photos to remind you of what it was like to be on the cusp of adolescence. The goal is to recall *what it felt like* to be a preteen and teenager, to remember how you felt and reacted, especially toward your parents.

Why Look Back?

The point of digging into your preteen past is to discover what kind of parent you are now and what kind of parent you want to be. Before we can change our parenting style, we need to see just where we are and why and how we got there. Many of us duplicate the good aspects of parenting that we picked up from our own parents. But we also repeat some of the negative styles without even thinking about them. Have you ever echoed your father's phrase "If all the other kids jumped off the bridge, would you jump, too?" Many of us have. We do not intend to replay those twenty- or thirty-year-old dialogues, but we do. They seem to fly off our lips before we can catch ourselves.

Take Jack, for instance. He is a loving father, a Saturday soccer coach, a good provider. Jack's own father was a critical man who always seemed to be checking on whether his children "measured up." One example was his considerable emphasis on their appearance: "Get a haircut. How can you go to school in those shabby clothes? Maybe you'd have decent friends if you looked better." His dad's frequent carping annoyed Jack throughout his adolescence, and he often swore to himself that he would never inflict such hurtful criticism on his own kids.

But one evening as she was heading out the door to meet friends, Jack's fourteen-year-old daughter, Lucia, bounced down the stairs in a short skirt and halter top.

"You're not going to wear *that*, are you?" Jack blurted. "Where did you get that outfit? Go back up and put on something else."

Lucia stomped up the stairs and returned moments later defiantly wearing baggy pants and a stained sweatshirt.

After Lucia left, Jack grinned sheepishly and said to his wife, "I didn't even realize what I was saying until I opened my mouth and my father came out."

It is not surprising that Jack and most parents repeat the same parenting styles—even the very words—that their parents used with them. Our parents were our primary models. We unconsciously learned how to be a parent from watching and interacting with them. Like Jack, many of us vow that we will not repeat the negative things that our parents said or did to us. But they slip out, especially when we are upset or caught off-guard by our kids.

Here's an exercise to help you keep that promise. Think about the most recent occasion when you repeated something that your parents used ineffectively or negatively with you. What steps do you think you can take to break that pattern, to prevent that from happening again? How could you handle a similar situation in the future so that it will have a more effective outcome? There are no right or wrong answers to these questions; just think about them.

On the other hand, our parents did not do such a bad job after all, did they? We survived. We even thrived. Despite our differences with them when we were teenagers, they did many things well. To appreciate their constructive efforts, try this mental exercise:

Think about the effective, positive things that your parents did when you were a teenager. Write them down. Talk to your brothers and sisters about them. If your parents are still living, talk to them about those things now.

Recall not only your parents' words and actions, but also the *feelings* you had as a teenager about your relationship with them:

- Did your parents listen to you? How did it feel when you knew they were really paying attention to your words?

- Did they make you feel comfortable and secure about bringing your problems and worries to them?

- Did they encourage you to express your emotions?

- How did they make you feel more confident about solving problems yourself?

Try to recall experiences when your parents did or said something that affected you in a *positive* way.

- What lesson did they teach you?

- How did they teach it?

- Why was it effective?

- Why do you think you still recall its impact today?

- How can you apply their positive technique to a specific situation with your own children today?

Remember, when I ask you to recall your own adolescence and think about your relationship with your parents, my goal is to help you consider and evaluate your own parenting style *now* with your own kids. When we look back at the environment in which we grew up, we can see where we are coming from. We can gain a better understanding of what kind of a parent we are, how we became that way, and if we are not satisfied with the parenting job that we are doing, how we may want to refashion our parenting style. So the questions now are: What kind of parent do I want to be now and in the future? What kind of relationship do I want to have with my children?

A key point: we have control over our parenting style. Although many of our parental impulses and reactions are influenced by the way our own parents raised us, we are not captives of the past. So do not just erase those old tapes in your head. Remember your parents' words and your memories of how they *felt*. Learn from your childhood tapes. Repeat the good parts.

And make the active decision not to repeat the other familiar, but uncomfortable, old scripts.

Avoid the Easy Pitfall— "I'll Just Be My Child's Friend."

All parents want to be loved. All parents want to be cool, especially if they were victims of uncool parents themselves. All parents want to have it easy. It often seems that one simple, effortless solution will guarantee that you are loved, assure you that you are considered cool, and head off any reason for your children to disagree with you—just be your child's friend. In fact, you might even be so cool that you will look like one of your child's friends. It is easy now with retro (a.k.a. "I'll just pull it out of my closet") fashions.

Please avoid this trap. Though it may make most days seem smoother, you will not be in a position of authority when you really need to make a strong decision. More important, if you try to become just like your adolescents, you will be making their developmental process of separation even more difficult. Remember that it's their job to become more independent of you. It is more helpful to them when they have a clear sense of what they are supposed to separate *from*.

Do not become a moving target: parental figure one moment, best pal the next. This will only frustrate them. Be cool by being consistent, always listening, not condemning, acknowledging that they need to grow, and all the while making sure that they are able to become their own person in a safe and responsible way.

Set Your Own Style

Throughout the rest of this book, your job is to tailor a variety of suggested skills and techniques to your own style and set of values. I do not intend to give you a philosophy or ethic for parenting. That is up to you. But I urge you to start this process by considering what your style and values are—and what you want them to be. Most parents do not think about them consciously or review them from time to time, so we slip up. We become inconsistent or wishy-washy about guiding our kids toward our values. That is why I strongly recommend that you take some time *this week* to examine your style, values, and goals. Try to step outside your skin and look at how you interact with your children, as if you were an impartial, invisible witness in your home. Some questions to ask yourself, and to discuss with your spouse:

- Do I like what I see and hear?

- Does it feel right?

- Is it working?

- Are we guiding our kids in positive directions? Or are they beginning to turn a deaf ear?

- Does my child feel that she can come to me no matter what, or do my reactions sometimes make her feel that she has made a mistake by coming to me?

- Does my child know that I will always find time to listen to him?

Now look at those answers through a broader perspective by considering both your disciplinary and emotional styles of parenting.

What Is Your Disciplinary Style?

Ask yourself and your partner questions like the following to identify where your parenting style falls on the strict-to-laid-back scale:

- Do I set high standards and expectations for my children's behavior, and do I let them know what those expectations are? Do I consistently enforce consequences when they break the rules? Do they see me as an authoritarian parent? Am I dogmatic?

- Do I have high expectations but also let my kids know that nobody is perfect? When they break the rules, do I listen to their explanations and come up with an appropriate consequence? Do I encourage them to solve their own problems, or do I hand them a solution?

- Do I let them do pretty much what they want? Is my philosophy that they will learn from their mistakes? If they lose their homework or a favorite jacket or a concert ticket, do I let them deal with the consequences themselves? Or do I bail them out?

- Do I let them talk me into bending the rules and letting them get out of a consequence? If we are a two-parent family, do my partner and I see eye-to-eye? Do we back each other up? Or do the kids know how to divide and conquer? If my spouse has denied them a privilege, do they come to me to get it reinstated? And how do I handle being caught in the middle?

What Is Your Emotional Style?

The previous questions mainly address how you tend to act and react when it comes to disciplinary situations. Now ask yourself some questions about your parenting style when it comes to *emotional issues* and how you communicate them.

- Do we talk about emotions in our family? Do we really listen to each other?

- When my children are upset, anxious, or angry, do I try to talk them out of those emotions? Or do I try to cheer them up and reassure them that the problem at hand will go away or improve? (Sometimes the most well-intentioned parents try to help a child by smoothing over problems when they actually could be more helpful by acknowledging the child's concerns and helping him develop skills to deal with those problems and emotions himself.)

- Do I listen and encourage them to express their feelings? Do I show them, by my own words and behavior, that it is OK to have a range of different, sometimes conflicting emotions?

- Do we talk about how emotions affect our actions—for example, do we acknowledge that it is normal and acceptable to be angry toward a brother who breaks our favorite toy, but it is not OK to punch him in the face for it? Do I help my children find ways to express emotions without hurting themselves or others?

- Do I send mixed emotional messages? Do I tell my daughter that I love her but say I am too busy to help her with her homework? Do I overreact with impatience or sarcasm when my kids make unintended mistakes?

Again, these questions are simply examples of ways to think about your parenting style. If you take a hard look at candid answers, you will start to think about your strengths and weaknesses. You can build on and reinforce your strengths and start to plan ways to change the weaknesses.

Are You a Really Good Listener?

The subject of listening will be repeated often in this book. Why? Because there is nothing more important to being an effective parent than your ability to listen and make your adolescent feel heard. When I ask virtually all teenagers about their relationships with parents, they respond almost uniformly, *"They don't listen to me."* Interestingly, the same adolescents' parents generally believe that they have made perfectly clear to their child that he or she can come to them for anything. Where is the breakdown in communication?

The reason that young people think their parents don't listen to them is really quite simple—*parents usually do not listen.* Rather, they react. Parents appropriately feel that it is their responsibility to guide, to teach, to fend off trouble. So as soon as they hear an alarm, they turn on lecture mode. (You'll find much more in Chapters 2 and 4 about why and how lectures not only do not work, they backfire.)

Do these scenarios sound familiar?

"Mom, I met this guy . . . "
"You're too young to date! Blah, blah, blah . . ."

"Dad, a bunch of the kids down at the pizza shop are
   smoking . . ."
"Don't you dare go to that pizza shop ever again! Blah,
   blah, blah . . ."

"Mom and Dad, Lisa has been teasing me . . ."
"She's just jealous of you! Blah, blah, blah . . ."

Do you see the problem here? The kids are opening up golden opportunities for discussion, perhaps about intimacy, avoiding harmful substances, or developing one's own self-esteem. But instead of listening to the child's joys, fears, and concerns, the parents jumped in with answers. Their answers either proclaim a new doctrine forbidding a certain behavior or offer a trite solution rather than allow the child to learn how to handle life's challenges. Do you see why adolescents decide just to stop talking?

In most of this chapter I have left the questions open-ended and suggested that you draw your own conclusions, but here I must be directive: Above all, you must learn how to be a good listener, an *active* listener. You must set a tone that makes your child feel he or she will never make a mistake by going to you to express anything.

Some hints:

1. Set some time aside, at least a couple of times a week, when you are not rushed and can be truly available to listen. (I know, it's easier said than done.)

2. Learn to turn off your parent alarm until you have heard the whole story.

3. Act interested in the subject matter because it is important to your child.

4. Learn to encourage expanded conversation by making neutral comments that do not betray your angst. Such comments might be "Really?" or "You've been giving this a lot of thought, huh?"

5. Before you share your wisdom—or even engage in the techniques that will be discussed in upcoming chapters—ask your child if he or she has any ideas about how best to handle the situation.

6. After hearing your child problem-solve, ask if you can share your thoughts. ("Would you like to hear an idea that just occurred to me?") You will find that having gained his permission to share your wisdom, your thoughts will not be rejected outright and maybe, just maybe, will even be respected.

Wouldn't it be wonderful if children came to us at perfect moments when we are relaxed, unhurried, and in a receptive mood to listen to them? Unfortunately, life is not always so neat. Kids' needs are not scheduled to be conveniently in sync with ours.

Many times a child wants to talk to Mom or Dad or ask questions when parents are distracted, busy, or interested in something else. For instance, their attention is focused on a breaking news story on TV or a friend who hasn't called in weeks suddenly phones—those may be precisely the times when children need to talk.

It is natural to say, "Wait. I'll be with you in a few minutes." And it is often necessary to put children's needs on hold. Parents should not be expected to drop everything at a child's whim. But I only caution you about postponing a chance to listen to your child: do it as sparingly as possible. Maybe the news on TV can wait. Perhaps you can call your friend back in an hour. Young adolescents' willingness to open up and talk to us is rare. If we do not pick up on these opportunities, they may not come again for a long while.

After you have spent some time thinking about your parenting style and values and have prepared yourself to be a more active listener, you will be ready to move on to learn more about how (not what) preteens and teenagers think. You may be in for some surprises.

2

How Preteens and Teens Think and Why That Matters

Adults make a lot of assumptions about young teenagers. We tend to believe that today's children are quite sophisticated. Through television, videos, movies, and the real-life experiences of families and friends, they have been exposed—some would say overexposed—to information, behaviors, events, and actions from which previous generations were sheltered.

Today many ten-year-olds know what a condom is and which friends' parents are having affairs, are alcoholics, use drugs, or abuse their families. Young people have a far more adult vocabulary than their parents did at the same age. They know the slang words for sex and drugs. They see sexually explicit scenes on soap operas, in movies and videos, and (despite parents' best efforts) many know how to skirt prohibitions on Internet access to X-rated language and behaviors.

This beyond-their-years exposure can be misleading. We think they actually know more than we did at their age. They may have witnessed more adult experiences and banter a more sophisticated language, but they don't necessarily *comprehend* more than previous generations did. In other words, quantity—more information—does not automatically translate into quality—perspective, responsibility, understanding, and judgment.

Why is that so? Developmentally, nine- to thirteen-year-olds have not yet acquired the intellectual or cognitive capability to process an onslaught of new information. They still think primarily in the same rigid good-or-bad, right-or-wrong terms as younger children. They live very much in the concrete here-and-now. And they have difficulty seeing future outcomes of current actions and decisions.

A simple example: If you offer a dollar bill to a six-year-old and say, "You can use this dollar to buy a candy bar or invest it in a retirement account at 7.5 percent interest, which will grow to thousands of dollars by the time you are sixty-five," you can well imagine which choice the child will make. He will not sit down, think it through carefully, calculate the compounded interest, and then weigh all that against the immediate gratification of how sweet the candy would taste. Instead, the dollar and the candy bar disappear quickly. All that is left is a smudge of chocolate on his fingers.

Children between ages nine and thirteen are still thinking very much like six-year-olds faced with this candy-or-investment decision. On their own, without our guidance and teaching, preteens do not yet make cognitive connections between present choices and long-term consequences. Their brains have not yet fully matured so they have not developed the intellectual capacity to think in abstract terms—to reason that if A and B occur, then C is likely to be the outcome.

Here's a common example of concrete thinking and its ramifications at this age:

At age twelve, Terese was diagnosed with asthma. Her doctor prescribed two different medications, both delivered by handheld inhalers. The first was to be used every day to *prevent* asthma attacks, and the second was to be used only when she wheezed or had trouble breathing. Although the doctor explained the difference to Terese, she stopped using the first inhaler after several weeks because she experienced no concrete effect. She used only the second inhaler when her asthma bothered her because it gave her immediate relief—she felt better right away. Health care professionals see this a great deal in young people with asthma. As they slow down or stop using preventive medications, they increase their use of others that give instant relief. In fact, they often overuse those inhalers precisely because they have stopped using the first type.

Parents confront a similar situation nearly every day when they try to get children to do homework. The parents know that completing these assignments leads to better grades, which leads to more academic opportunities and career achievements in the years ahead. But when Mom or Dad are reminding them to finish their homework, kids think only in terms of the immediate future: "I really wish I could be outside playing basketball or watching that TV show."

Inside the Brain, a Work-in-Progress

Between childhood and adolescence, we can actually see our children's bodies grow and change. Sometimes it seems to happen overnight or over a summer vacation. Their limbs lengthen and their muscles increase. A child's physical growth is unveiled right before our eyes between ages nine and fourteen. We watch and are amazed. We may wonder, does cognitive development run parallel to physical growth during these years? How does a child's ability to think, reason, and comprehend develop during the preteen years?

Cognitive development is much more difficult to gauge than physical growth during these years. Parents often wish they could see inside the brain of a twelve-year-old so that they might better understand why this child can act so mature and responsible one day and then regress to a whiny, unreasonable toddler the next. Because we cannot see inside their heads, the only way to attempt to measure their intellectual development is to study their words and actions.

Recent science and technology are just beginning to reveal some fascinating new information about how the young brain grows and develops. This field is still in its infancy, but early information seems to paint a picture that explains much of the inconsistent behaviors we observe. Certainly more will be known in the near future.

The brain of a young person is a work-in-progress—tremendous progress. The period between ages nine or ten and early adolescence is marked by dramatic neurological growth and change. The only other time in life when the human brain achieves such strides is the period soon after infancy.

Think of the brain in computer terms for a moment. The neural circuitry is like hardware, but it is not completely installed in most youths until their early twenties. The installation process is neither smooth nor uniform because different regions of the brain are maturing at different paces. One of the last areas to become fully developed, in fact, is the region that regulates decision making and tempers emotions. Keep that in mind when your child explodes one morning with "Get off my back! I hate you!" and cuddles up next to you that evening and asks for help with homework.

The brain's important prefrontal cortex is like the executive suite where judgments are made and emotions are regulated. It operates pretty much as it has since early childhood. That is, it has not fully swung into action. It is not completely ready or able to make complex, mature judgments during the preteen years.

But the area of the brain where emotions originate is about to take off like a rocket. It is called the limbic system. Located deep inside the brain, it sends out gut reactions such as anger and fear. You can imagine the result when these two separate parts of the brain are developing at different paces. Here are two examples that might sound familiar to you:

It's 9:30 P.M. and eleven-year-old Sondra suddenly remembers that her Spanish test is tomorrow morning. She has not cracked the book or looked at a vocabulary list. Sondra goes into a panic, crying and wailing that she will fail sixth grade and be a total failure in life.

Or ten-year-old William flares up at the kid on the bus who called him a wuss in front of his friends. He swears he is going to smash the boy's face before school tomorrow. He does not weigh the fact that the boy is four inches taller and twenty pounds heavier.

Sondra and William's prefrontal cortexes have not yet developed enough to say, "Chill out. Life won't come crashing down if you fail a test or another kid belittles you. You'll figure out a way to get through this." Instead, their brains' limbic systems are going full blast, sending out gut reactions like fear, anxiety, and anger without the counterbalance that a more mature prefrontal cortex could provide.

A Scientific Snapshot

Cutting-edge research and technology using magnetic resonance imaging (MRI) to take pictures of brain activity have begun to show us how young brains work differently from mature ones. For example, in one study teens and adults were shown pictures of human faces twisted in fright. Then they were asked to name the emotion. All the adults said "fear," but many of the teenagers were unable to identify the expression. The researchers, Deborah Yurgelun-Todd and Abigail Baird at McLean Hospital in Boston, used MRI to see which parts of the brain were being used as both adults and teenagers looked at the pictures.

Both the limbic areas and the prefrontal cortex lit up in the adults' brains. But in the teenage brains, the limbic system lit up while the prefrontal cortex remained mainly dark. Conclusion: young brains are not as able to interpret expressions or read social signals as well as adult brains because their prefrontal cortexes are not fully mature.

Until fairly recently, the human brain was believed to reach adulthood soon after puberty. Now research is revealing new evidence that the prefrontal cortex hits a growth spurt near puberty. Neurons begin to make new connections, or *synapses*, like multiplying rabbits.

Many of these new links die off in a process called *pruning* after about age eleven in girls and twelve in boys. This allows the brain to nourish only the useful neurons and synapses so that the brain can think more efficiently. This process has been called *streamlining* by neuroscientists involved in several research projects around the country. They believe that the streamlining process continues into young adulthood.

Although the preteen brain has not achieved its full ability to make mature, sound, and responsible judgments, do not be discouraged—*good judgment can be taught and practiced.* The dawning of adolescence marks the time when one *begins* to have the capability to think abstractly, but the system has to be greased with experiences.

That is what this book is all about. I want to give you skills and techniques to help your child navigate these years of developing brain power, but it is essential that you appreciate the basic biological foundation first: the hardware is not fully installed yet, so you need to understand and support the child through these ups and downs *by structuring experiences* that teach the lessons you want them to learn.

Brain Chemistry, Hormones, and Nerves

Three more pieces of this puzzle are important to recognize before we move forward. First, brain chemistry is changing during these years. Various chemicals are achieving a new balance that affects electrical impulses passing along nerve fibers. The second piece of the puzzle involves sex hormones coursing through your child's bloodstream. They influence not only sexual development, but also the brain's maturation. The effects of testosterone and estrogen in puberty have been likened to "flipping neurological switches" that were set while the child was still developing in utero. When those switches are flipped, they affect a teenager's emotions and sex drive as well as mental skills.

The third piece of the puzzle concerns nerve coating. A waxy substance called *myelin* coats nerves and acts like insulation on an electric cord. Myelin permits electrical impulses to speed along a nerve quickly and efficiently. But a baby is not born with all his or her myelin in place. It takes two decades for the nervous system to complete myelination. That is part of the reason why a five-year-old is more clumsy than his twelve-year-old brother who, in turn, is not as well coordinated as he will be when he is eighteen.

During the teen years, many nerves in the parts of the brain that determine impulse control, emotion, and judgment are still not fully sheathed in myelin as they will be when the child reaches adulthood. When we parents realize how dramatically the brain is developing, we are struck by how the mind's great potential can be influenced by the right environment and by "exercising" it appropriately. It also makes it all the more scary to think about harmful effects on that development, such as doing drugs.

Now that you have come through the above neurobiology lesson with flying colors, let me sum up some basic points: Your child's brain is changing rapidly but not on a steady keel. As the hard-wiring gets installed, expect ups and downs—emotional highs and lows, surprising intellectual insights counterbalanced by some truly immature, dumb decisions. Keep in mind that your child *will* eventually achieve higher mental skills, better judgment, and more responsible decision-making skills. He or she will be able to control impulses and grasp more abstract, cause-and-effect concepts.

But until then, do not expect young teens to think logically. If you try to reason with them that smoking tobacco, for example, is harmful to their health, they will not envision themselves wheezing, coughing, and possibly having lung cancer or heart disease by midlife.

A child who is offered a cigarette does not think, "Gee, this contains highly addictive nicotine. I might get hooked. If I smoke for ten or twenty years, I could get lung cancer." This child is still thinking concretely and only in the present moment, so she thinks, "Yeah, I'll try it. My friends have smoked. It looks cool." Or she may say to herself, "It makes my parents mad when I smoke, and I like that attention" or "It makes them think I'm grown up." Or perhaps she has seen her parents smoking, modeling the very same behavior they caution her against, but one that they say helps them relax. In each case, the immediate benefit is clear to any young teen. It is easy to grasp. It is tangible. It is *concrete*.

An adult's abstract thinking is highly protective. A child's concrete thinking is not. She does not yet think about future consequences of current behavior. Lung cancer? To twelve-year-olds, it's a cool name for a punk rock band.

Even if they understood the ramifications of lung cancer or emphysema, those diseases happen to old people. They think, "We are not old, so what's the problem?" Either they cannot imagine they will ever be old, or they are certain that they will quit smoking before they grow old or get sick. A vague outcome fifty years down the road does not even begin to match the immediate thrills of doing something that they know makes adults crazy. Get it? In this case, the only way to prevent adolescent smoking is not by delivering an abstract, reasoned lecture filled with future threats, but by making young teens aware of the concrete, immediate problems with smoking—stinky breath and hair, yellow teeth, the high cost of tobacco.

As adults we often wish that a preteen would only "listen to reason." His ears may hear our words, but his brain does not process our well-reasoned message. An adult's sound logic concludes that an unchaperoned party is an open invitation to trouble—perfectly reasonable to a parent, right? We know what can happen: Older kids could stop by, bring beer and marijuana. Younger kids might get into a car with an older teen who has been drinking. And then there are those empty bedrooms with no adult in the house. Any parent can envision all the scary scenarios.

Young teens do not think that way. They do not envision and weigh the wide array of possible outcomes. They simply think that the party will be a chance to have fun, to be with friends, to be accepted, to act more grown up, to taste a little freedom. If you question the wisdom of going to this party, you will probably get answers like "Everybody's going . . . There won't be any trouble . . . I can handle it . . . Don't you trust me?" They may even sincerely believe that they will "just say no" to trouble and that you should believe in their ability to "handle it" as deeply as they believe in it themselves. Yet they may find themselves unprepared for the array of manipulations that other people may use to get them to "just say yes."

Thanks for the Cookie

Here's one more central point to keep in mind as your child's cognitive abilities start to mature: Preteens still think much like younger children when it comes to people and their motivations. They judge another person as good or bad depending on how that person treats them. Adults, thinking in the abstract and considering various possibilities and future consequences, realize that another person may treat them well but harbor underlying selfish motives.

Children have not yet acquired this protective way of thinking. If a five-year-old is offered a chocolate chip cookie, she thinks that the giver is a good person: "Someone who does a nice thing must be nice, right? I should do what nice adults ask me!" That is one of the reasons childhood can be so dangerous. The vast majority of young children and preteens have not had enough life experiences to learn that people may have other motives that are not always benevolent. That is why we teach young children not to fall for the "please hop in my car and help me find my lost puppy" line of a total stranger.

Now let me ask you: if someone takes you out to the nicest dinner (the adult equivalent of a cookie) and then asks you something inappropriate, do you say, "Well, sure, you are so kind"? You are less vulnerable as an adult.

In the earliest years, learning from life experiences usually is not too dangerous because most young children are protected by parents and other adults. We are with them more often, looking over their shoulders, catching them before they fall, preventing real dangers for the most part. But as they enter early adolescence, there is less adult on-site protection.

Life experiences are great, effective teachers. But as we have seen, we cannot afford to let children mess up and learn entirely from their own mistakes because today's risks are too dangerous. For adolescents, learning a lesson from life experiences often comes with the high cost of being manipulated by others. A young teen who cannot read another's motivations may very well end up hurt, harmed, or worse. Here is an example of a life experience lesson that is all too common:

A sixteen-year-old boy tells fourteen-year-old Sara, "I love you."

Sara does not ask herself rationally, "I question that. How do I know he means it?"

More typically, Sara will take his words at face value. "Oh, wow! He loves me," she thinks. "It's love! It has finally happened to me! It feels so good to have a guy love me."

(Do you recall how easily you fell in love the first time? For me, it happened when I returned from an absence in fifth grade to discover that a girl in my class—a girl eight inches taller than me yet!—had moved our desks together because she liked me. Well, if she liked me, then I was in love!)

He follows up with, "And when you're in love, you show each other by doing it. I love you and I want to have sex with you."

Sara thinks, "I guess I'm in love. My mother told me to make sure to wait for a special someone. I've finally found him! I guess this is what we'll do, like I've seen on TV." So they have sex after school before her parents come home. The next day the boy is out of her life. He passes her on the street and ignores her. A few days later, Sara sees him with another girl. She is crushed. Yes, Sara has learned a hard lesson from real-life experience: *People do not always mean what they say. They say certain things to manipulate us to get what they want.*

Because our preteens appear to be more worldly than previous generations, we may presume that they are savvy enough to see a manipulative line for what it is, or to judge a person's character or motivation with some accuracy. But they are not. Again, their brains are not fully mature and their life experiences have not yet burned them (we hope), so kids this age continue to view people in fairly simplistic, good-or-bad terms. It is important to keep this in mind because this still-immature way of thinking leaves them highly vulnerable.

In Sara's case she made what she thought was a well-reasoned decision: "He loves me. He seems to care. I was waiting for someone to be in love with. Now is the time." This experience has indeed moved her a step toward safety. She may have become aware of a line for the first time and may harbor a more healthy suspicion in the future. She will not fall for the "I love you" line again. But is she ready for other lines? She has moved a step toward the safety of adulthood, but she will have to make a series of other mistakes, each time gaining a bit of wisdom until she can negotiate life as a protected adult.

"What!?" you are asking yourself. "He's saying this has made her move a step closer to safety? What about the fact that she has been emotionally hurt? That she might be pregnant or have a disease?" Precisely. We cannot allow our kids to learn from mistakes, despite how effective and efficient "real experiences" can be in moving them toward safer behaviors later. Instead, we want to make them aware of problems *before* they occur (as will be discussed in Chapter 4), and we want them to know in advance how to recognize and respond to a line (Chapter 5).

Morals and Rules

We have just examined young teenagers' cognitive development, but before we move ahead to learn specific ways to guide and influence them, it is important to consider their moral and psychological development as well. Let me sum it up briefly. In the early years, children's moral decisions are based on their desire to avoid punishment or not get caught. They see something as morally wrong only if it will produce a bad outcome for them. "If my parents don't know I did it, then I did nothing wrong" is the typical line of thinking at this age. For the same reason, they sometimes lie to avoid consequences or punishment.

I remember an instance when one of my daughters really wanted to eat a long-stem chocolate rose that I'd bought for her for Valentine's Day. My wife and I cruelly suggested that she wait until after she ate dinner. Four-year-old Talia sat on the steps with a door pulled open in front of her. She could not see us, so she assumed that we could not see her. It produced one of my favorite pictures—a great photo of her from the neck down with a chocolate stem sticking out from the door that covered her face. From Talia's point of view, if she wasn't caught, then she did nothing wrong. You can see how an early adolescent with the same philosophy might just get in trouble.

Fortunately, by adolescence most children move beyond this stage and begin to develop a more conventional morality. Their decisions are now based on their desire to be viewed as a good person. Early on, the criterion of *good* is determined by their parents' definition. It becomes more complex later when peers begin to define what is good.

A story involving my other daughter illustrates a young child's interpretation of *good* this way: "As long as my Mommy says I am still good, if I do something, I am good." When Ilana was four, she came to my wife, Celia, with a cassette tape whose innards were hanging out. She confessed to Celia that she might have been there when the cassette broke. Celia very clearly made the point that she was so proud of Ilana for coming to her and telling the truth. Accidents happen and, in fact, Ilana was a very *good* girl. The broken tape meant nothing compared to how good she had been in telling the truth.

The next day Celia was sitting on the front porch with a neighbor when Ilana came out and asked, "Mommy, would you be mad if the glass chimes broke?"

Celia reinforced the same point: "Of course not. Not if you told me."

"OK."

"Is there something you'd like to tell me?" Celia queried. "Did the chimes break?"

"No, really," replied my little lady. "I just wanted to check if you'd be mad if I broke them."

Ilana went back inside. Celia was a bit disappointed that Ilana did not yet feel comfortable enough to tell the truth but felt satisfied that she had taught the lesson. Suddenly, Celia heard our other daughter yelling frantically, "Ilana, if you keep swinging a stick at them, they really will break!"

From Ilana's point of view, she had just come to Mommy to get permission to break the chimes and to make sure she was still good if she did break them!

Moral development does not stop there. The next step usually occurs in adolescence when young people begin to recognize the rule of law. They realize that rules are made for social order. In fact, they might rigidly adhere to rules and regulations. Later in adolescence, they remain interested in social order, but they begin to accept the complexity of moral questions. They start to wonder about moral relativity, hypocrisy, and extenuating circumstances. You will know when your child reaches this stage because every decision you make will need lots of explanation, and you will hear a great deal about extenuating circumstances that you just do not understand. Do not be shocked if you even are accused of hypocrisy—I've heard rumors that adolescents sometimes do that.

Some older teens achieve a level of morality at which they strive for higher moral standards than the general society. When they reach this level, many young people take high moral stands, such as boycotting companies that pollute the environment, protesting human rights violations, vowing never to eat anything that had a mother, and opposing war.

Evolving Independence

Another important fact to keep in mind as your preteen moves into adolescence is that the fundamental job of all teenagers is to become independent. They must increasingly reject your supervision, your advice, and even your values. As rocky as this path can become for both teen and parent, remember that your child is not arguing with you because she hates you. She may say she does. She may scream, "You're so stupid. No other parent in the world is as mean as you are!" Or, it is typical for preteens to tell a parent emphatically, "I don't need you!" They do need you, of course, but they often say this to draw you into a conflict in order to grab your attention.

In reality, young teens feel very close to their parents although they are uncomfortable about it. They still love and need the security of their families, but they also sense a growing need to pull away, to explore who they are, who they want to be, where and how they will fit in. As adolescents seem to reject their parents, they begin to forge new families—a circle of friends. The push and pull toward growing independence is at the heart of a teenager's vulnerability to peer pressure.

3

Behavioral Change— Step by Step

As children move toward adolescence, parents often ask themselves, "How can I know that my son or daughter won't become involved in worrisome, even dangerous, behaviors? What can I do to be sure my child will grow up to be safe, responsible, and happy?"

I wish there were easy answers. I wish that I could fill these pages with foolproof recipes for success. Clearly, parenting adolescents is not simple. Any expert who implies it is easy only sets parents up for frustration. And make no mistake about it, if I—a guy who thinks he knows enough about parenting to write a book about it—moved into your home and tried to coparent with you, I would also struggle and sometimes feel inadequate. Even the best parents find young teens to be challenging.

Yet anyone who tells you that parents have *no* influence sets you up for unnecessary failure. *The truth is, we adults cannot control our adolescents' behavior, but we certainly can influence it.*

Most theories about influencing or changing behavior have at their core five sequential steps. Whether the goal is to eliminate a problem behavior (for example, stop underage drinking), to redirect a negative behavior to a positive one (leave a group of delinquent friends and hang out with others who have a healthier influence), or to adopt an entirely new, constructive behavior (getting terrific grades), the same series of steps is essential:

STEP 1—Becoming aware that a problem or situation exists

STEP 2—Recognizing that the problem affects you so that you become motivated to change

STEP 3—Learning and using appropriate skills to work toward a solution

STEP 4—Weighing the costs and benefits of changing the behavior

STEP 5—Making and sticking to the decision whether or not to adopt the change

These steps are linked like rings in a chain. They constitute a five-stage *process*: each one is necessary to the next step. We adults typically approach behavioral change naively when we try to influence adolescents. We tell them what to do. That technique is guaranteed to fail. It not only does not work, but it actually backfires quite often.

If we wish to influence any adolescent behavior—either turn around a negative one or initiate a positive one—we first need to figure out where a child is along this five-step path. Is she entirely unaware of the problem? Does she know it exists but cannot imagine it happening to her? Does she want to adopt a more responsible behavior or avoid a risky one but does not have the skills to do so? Or is she approaching the problem with faulty skills? Has she tried out a solution but now needs to weigh the costs and benefits before deciding whether the behavioral change is worth it? Is she teetering on the brink of deciding whether the new action is worth maintaining permanently?

After figuring out which stage your child is in and which one she needs to advance past, it is time to put our strategy into place. Our immediate goal is to support her in succeeding at this current step. Our long-term strategy is to put into place the ingredients that will support her through the entire five-step process.

As you begin this process, do not assume that your child is at the same step for every situation. Young adolescents often are at different stages for different problems at any given moment. Your strategy therefore may need to change depending on the problem at hand. Take Michael, for example, who is at different steps for two separate situations:

Michael knows that drugs are a serious problem. He is past Step 1. He also may not want drugs to affect his athletic performance, so he is motivated to avoid them. He is past Step 2. But what if he has no idea about how to deal with peer pressure to experiment with drugs? He will need help developing such skills (Step 3).

A different situation, same young man: Michael knows the danger of head injuries that can result from biking (past Step 1). He experienced injury firsthand when he flipped off his bike and broke his arm last summer (past Step 2). He has the skill to put on a helmet with ease (past Step 3). He likes the fact that he feels protected in the helmet (a Step 4 benefit). But Michael does not appreciate that benefit enough to be willing to deal with the grief that he gets from friends for looking uncool in a helmet (a Step 4 cost).

Whether Michael adopts the behavior change (Step 5) of consistently wearing a helmet may be determined by the amount of reinforcement he gets from both his parents and the peers he admires most, the serious mountain bikers. Let's look at the five steps in closer detail.

Step 1

Becoming aware of a real problem or a situation that may become either dangerous or beneficial is the critical first step in positive behavioral change. Without this first step, a child cannot hope to move forward. If your daughter had no awareness that improved school performance is a desirable behavior that is somehow rewarded in real life, why would she work harder in class? Why would she decide to avoid drugs when her friends tell her that they are fun if she does not know that they also can be harmful?

Adults spend most of their effort trying to move kids through Step 1. In fact, we tend to think that as long as we make them aware, we have solved the problem. We assume they will have the good sense to make the smart choices and do the right thing. We lecture them and tell them what to do. Or we sometimes only tell them that something is a problem "because I said so!"

Step 2

At Step 2, a young person has to move beyond simple awareness to realize that a problem can have a direct, personal effect.

As long as the problem belongs to someone else, there is no reason or incentive for the child to act on it. ("Hey, it's her problem, not mine" or "Other people get hooked on drugs but I can handle it" or "People who look dirty carry HIV, not the people I hang around with" or "Bob tells me he is a careful driver when he drinks. I know that drinking is unsafe while driving, but he would never hurt me.")

Although many youths (and adults) use denial to feel safer in the world, we tend to overestimate the extent to which teens feel invulnerable. There's a popular myth out there that young people actually think they are invulnerable ("It'll never happen to me."). They may behave that way or project that attitude because that is the appearance they want to project to their peers, but in fact, they worry quite a bit. It is critical to remember this because if we try to drive home a teenager's vulnerability constantly, it can backfire by producing even higher stress. A far more effective approach is to motivate them to move beyond awareness of a problem and take the next of the five sequential steps—acquiring skills, weighing costs and benefits, and making a decision to make a change in behavior.

Step 3

The development of skills (Step 3) is pivotal in determining whether an individual has the ability to change. Without specific skills to avoid a problem or deal with peers, an adolescent is easily swayed to engage in risky behaviors. And without skills to adopt positive behaviors—like studying—a teenager is unable to reach desired goals. So even after a child becomes aware of a situation and is highly motivated to do something about it, he will only become frustrated if he lacks the skills to take action.

On the other hand, action is not always beneficial. One danger of adolescence is teens' tendency to employ harmful skills. They may choose a course of action to avoid a problem, but the choice may bring more harm than good. For example, young people are very worried about violence. They take active steps to stay safe. Some teens are wise and choose to avoid conflicts, but others want to feel protected and decide to carry weapons, which contributes to *less* safety for themselves, their schools, and their communities.

Step 4

At Step 4, costs and benefits of a particular action or choice are measured. Something is usually given up in order to gain something else. A teen who quits smoking, for example, gains several benefits: breathing better, avoiding yellow teeth, losing the stale smoky odor on clothes and hair, and saving money. But he gives up some things, too: looking rebellious and having the instant relaxation that comes with smoking. The teenager who studies harder gains the benefit of higher grades and parental satisfaction but gives up free time to hang out with friends.

It's critical to understand that many of the behaviors we consider negative also carry some benefit for teenagers ("Smoking relaxes me. It helps me chill out."). So we need to encourage young people to replace those "benefits" with others that carry stronger, healthier benefits (such as, "Have you figured out how much exercise can help you relax?"). If we can show them constructive alternatives, they will have the opportunity to learn that the cost of negative behaviors outweighs the short-term benefits.

Step 5

Finally, when a teenager arrives at Step 5, she has to decide whether or not to adopt a new behavior or drop an established one permanently. She is now aware, personally motivated, has acquired the skills, and has determined that the benefits would be more valuable than the costs. Now she is ready to decide whether to adopt the new behavior.

What's the determining factor? Whether she chooses and sticks to this new behavior depends on the *reinforcement* she receives from parents, teachers, peers, and other people who are important to her. Not all of those people, of course, will reinforce behaviors in the same way. For any given behavior, reinforcement can go in opposite directions: Parents might support studying while the peer group might support cutting classes. Or an older sibling might tell her, "I think it's cool that you are saving yourself for the person you will marry," while a classmate might say, "What? You haven't even done it yet?"

A Slam Dunk Proposition

To illustrate just how complex behavioral change can be, here is what should be a slam dunk proposition: "Wear a helmet when you skate." No matter how much parents try to influence their child with reasonable explanations, cajoling, or demanding, their son may take his helmet off when he is out of their presence. Even after they have made him aware of the dangers of skating without it, have motivated him to wear it, and provided the skill (by buying an attractive, easy to strap on, comfortable helmet), he still may get stuck at Step 4—weighing the costs and benefits.

The young teen recognizes the obvious benefit—avoiding brain injury—but he also sees the cost as no longer looking carefree and daring to his friends or losing the immediate pleasure of the wind blowing through his hair. The benefits are a no-brainer to an adult, but the teenager sees the dramatic benefit—you'll live if you crash or get hit!—as irrelevant to him. He thinks, "Everyone I know skates without a helmet. They all seem to be alive."

Even if he thinks the benefits outweigh the costs, he ultimately may decide *not* to make a helmet his habit. Why? Because at Step 5, people look for reinforcement—encouragement or discouragement from family or friends—to stick with the new behavior. Whether this boy will consistently wear his helmet or continue to disregard it will depend on how accepting his crowd of friends is. His parents could step in by taking him to "Skater Heaven" where helmets are mandated rather than let him practice skating in the street. They might also buy him the coolest-looking helmet, which will make him the envy of his friends.

Ultimately though, the situation may be outside his parents' control. It may require something like a massive marketing campaign to make bike or skate helmet use the "in" thing, to create an environment where safety will be reinforced. But making helmet use "in" is not a pie-in-the-sky dream. Consider what has happened to the perception of drinking and driving since we were in high school. Public health campaigns successfully made it cool to have designated drivers and uncool to let your friends drive drunk. Do not overlook this point: your power as a parent to influence children's behavior may involve advocating for the right thing in your community or in the media.

A Basic Foundation

This chapter has deliberately been brief because I want it to provide a basic foundation for the remainder of the book. The five sequential steps that I have described to effect behavioral change will be expanded upon in the remaining chapters, but I want you to have an overview now—a roadmap, so to speak—to give you an idea of the direction we need to take in order to teach skills and strategies and continually reinforce desired behaviors (as well as to avoid negative ones) throughout adolescence.

Chapter 4 will offer techniques to help your child become aware of problems and consider the consequences. It will demonstrate that lectures in the traditional sense do not work, but other approaches (role-playing, decision trees, choreographed discussions, modeling) can help get across the same lessons more effectively. Chapter 5 will guide you in developing your child's ability to deal with and resist peer pressure. Chapter 6 will discuss stress and how it can lead young people toward negative coping behaviors, which they see as having short-term benefits. We will present constructive alternatives to prevent or help them get unstuck from destructive patterns. Chapter 7 will help you reinforce positive behaviors by creating a strong, wide network of peers, older teens, and other adults. Chapter 8 will redefine *discipline* as it is usually understood and dispensed. By giving children plenty of positive attention, you can actively guide them toward appropriate behaviors and diminish negative punishments. Chapter 9 addresses the type of loving guidance that helps your child become gradually more independent while staying safe at the same time. And Chapter 10 discusses the most important reinforcement you can possibly offer your child—a deep, loving connection with you.

You will encounter several new terms (decision trees, choreographed conversations, cognitive Ah-ha!) in the next few chapters as well as others (like role-playing) that may be familiar. All of these techniques can broaden your repertoire of parenting skills, but I urge you not to use these approaches in a rigid, mechanistic way. If you try to memorize them or incorporate them into nearly every conversation with your child, you will come across as a robot. Your child will easily detect that you are trying too hard, and your relationship will become strained and stiff. The natural spontaneity of interacting with your child comfortably will evaporate. I hope you will use these special techniques *at key points* when you need to teach specific lessons or give critical information. Learn these techniques, but try not to overuse them. They are designed to prepare you to help your children come to their own conclusions while you avoid the alienating lecture. And remember, the most important skills are the easiest ones: listening to your child and communicating in clear, concrete language.

4

Better Ways to Make Your Child Aware of Consequences

As we have seen on the previous pages and in real life, preteens do not make decisions the same way adults do because they are not yet able to think in abstract terms, weigh various possibilities, and predict future outcomes of present actions. But young adolescents are not oversized children either. If we want to guide and communicate with them effectively, we cannot treat them like little kids. Edicts like "Because I said so" will no longer work. They want us to talk to them with respect. They expect us to trust them. Preteens want us to treat them like young adults even if they are not yet.

When they challenge us with back talk or undesirable behaviors, we sometimes forget this important fact: Young adolescents very much want to please their parents. Oh, they will never say that aloud, but during these preteen years, you have a golden opportunity to capitalize on their affection and desire to please you. You can use your position to guide and to teach because they are listening and watching. The trick, though, is to be subtle about it.

Our challenge is to walk this fine line: to support their appropriate behaviors with respect and caring, while also recognizing the limits of their cognitive ability at this age. We need to teach them a wide variety of thinking and coping skills so that they will be armed with an arsenal of constructive alternatives to risky behaviors and unwise decisions. That is what we will discuss in this chapter and the following. But first, it is necessary to consider what doesn't work with preteens. Before we can substitute constructive ways to guide them, we need to break some old, ineffective patterns.

Does this scenario sound familiar?

Ricky wants to spend Sunday at his friend's house. He has not raked the backyard—one of his regular weekend chores—or completed the homework assignment that is due Monday morning. His room is strewn with comic books, empty juice cans, grungy socks, and tee shirts, yet Ricky implores his father for a ride to Sam's house.

"No, you can't go," his dad says.

"Why not?"

"Because your room is a mess."

"I'll clean it up tonight."

"You have homework to finish tonight."

"I'll do it later. Now please drive me over to Sam's house."

"No, in fact, I ought to punish you for not doing your chores."

"Awww, come on, Dad." Ricky's voice rises and he begins pacing angrily.

"NO!"

"Why not? You're so mean!"

"Don't talk back to me. I said no, and I mean no."

"But I want to go. I'm going to go. Sam's waiting for me."

"Don't defy me. You can't go because I said so. Now, go to your room!"

We know where this is going. Ricky is thinking and behaving like the typical eleven-year-old that he is. His brain is not ready to prioritize, think things through carefully, and discover that what he wants can be achieved if he figures out a rational way to schedule his chores and do his homework.

Ricky is not thinking abstractly. He does not consider possibilities and reach rational conclusions. His thoughts are not: "If I quickly toss my dirty laundry in the hamper, stack the comic books under my bed, and put the cans in the recycling bucket, that will take about ten minutes. Then if I rake the yard for twenty minutes, I can convince Dad to let me go to Sam's for the afternoon. That'll leave me two hours after supper to finish my homework."

Instead, Ricky's brain is thinking in concrete, black-and-white terms in the here and now: "I want what I want. I want it now. Dad's not budging. He's mean. I hate his guts." In other words, Ricky still thinks very much like a five-year-old. The emotional center of his brain is outpacing the rational part.

The exchange between Ricky and his father is fairly common and benign. Whether Ricky picks up his room or finishes his homework will not matter very much in ten years. Their argument will blow over in a day or so, but Ricky will not have moved any closer to thinking in an abstract, cause-and-effect manner because his dad and he are on parallel tracks that will never meet. His father has not approached his son at Ricky's cognitive level. He has not helped Ricky step out of the concrete thinking box.

Let's fast-forward this scene a couple of years and ratchet up the situation. Ricky is now sixteen and the confrontation concerns his coming home drunk with a dent in Dad's car. It is easy to see how Dad's style will not work. It is doomed to fail. Yelling, punishing, threatening, and lecturing will only make Ricky defensive and angry toward his father. The incident will not teach Ricky any useful lesson or make him take responsibility for his actions.

The Futility of Lecturing

It is easy to fall into a pattern of lecturing. Most parents do it. We see a problem, our parent alarm switches on, and we launch into lecture mode. Parents typically think: "I'll share my wisdom. If I only give him enough solid reasons, he'll see it my way and behave the way I want him to."

Think about what a lecture really is: a series of statements, often combined subtly or not so subtly with threats. We explain how the choice of action A will lead to consequence B, which in turn could lead to consequence C, or ultimately ruin the child's life through consequence D. But there are at least three problems with the lecture approach:

1. A parent usually begins a lecture before the young person has had a chance to complete a thought or express a concern, so the child feels unheard.

2. Lectures are usually given without the child's permission to intervene, so the child feels intruded upon and disrespected.

3. Lectures are abstract in nature, as they move from consequence to consequence. The lecturer presumes

that preteens understand future consequences of each behavior, which we know is actually beyond their cognitive ability. Because young teens cannot do this, they feel stupid.

For all of the above reasons, lecturing is not only ineffective, it backfires. When people feel unheard, intruded upon, disrespected, and, in particular, are made to feel stupid, is it any wonder that they become defensive and hostile? Even if preteens sulk away and do not become angry, they are still incapable of incorporating parental wisdom.

Do you remember how adults talked in *Peanuts* cartoons? *Wha wa, wha wa, wha wa, wha wa . . .* That is what adolescents hear when we lecture them. If you do not believe it, just watch their eyes lose focus when you move beyond your first point or two of a lecture.

When I say "Do not lecture," I mean that in the traditional, long-winded, behind-the-podium sense. I want to be very clear about this: I am not advising you against conveying information. But I strongly urge you to learn to *convey information in a manner that will be effective and not alienating.* You could say that I want to show you how to lecture in a different way. In the rest of this chapter I will explain several ways to convey the same information that you would try to get across in a lecture, but these alternatives are reframed in ways that a preteen can hear, comprehend, and use.

Ah-Ha!

I have coined the term *cognitive Ah-Ha!* to describe our ultimate goal in guiding children actively through the process of moving from concrete to abstract thinking. We want to bring preteens to the point of "getting it," of absorbing the information we want to get across, by reaching their own solutions. And when they do, the light bulb will switch on: "Ah-Ha! I see!" This is particularly useful in moving young people through the first two steps of behavioral change—awareness and motivation.

We do this by creating cognitive Ah-Ha! experiences. We will steer preteens verbally through "life experiences" and allow them to make "mistakes" in the safety of our home and family environments. We will stage-manage these life experiences, so to speak, in the hope that the unwise choices they make in these verbal rehearsals will spark realizations about what those same mistakes can cost in the outside, dangerous world.

The key to this style of guidance lies in *breaking down abstract concepts into simple, clear, concrete parts—in sequence— one step after another.* (You're not allowed to skip steps or jump ahead! If your child gets stuck on one step, go back and come at it from another angle, with another example perhaps.) We will guide them, as a director might guide actors through play rehearsals, step by step, or line by line, until they reach an abstract realization—"Ah-Ha! Now I get it!" Or, if you prefer sports analogies, think of this process as bringing them down the football field, yard by yard, until they reach the end zone. When they reach the goal, their eyes light up with sudden comprehension—"Ah-Ha!"

The following strategies (role-playing, decision trees, choreographed discussions, and modeling) will illustrate ways to create cognitive Ah-Ha! experiences for your young teens. As you start to think about this process, here are three ground rules to remember:

1. Keep it simple

2. Keep it concrete

3. Keep your focus on two basic concepts:
   - the consequences of behaviors
   - other people's underlying motivation

As you learn how to transform abstract concepts into concrete information, you will be using techniques that build on children's own strengths. The concepts and lessons will be easier for them to grasp when you construct them around familiar, everyday experiences.

Role-Playing

This is not about putting on a costume or getting up on a stage. *Role-playing* is a fairly simple way of showing children how to think through various situations by stepping out of their own shoes and into someone else's and by using their imagination to think of alternative actions and behaviors to get out of a jam. It is a safe way to practice scenarios that could become harmful. And it is a way to apply practical strategies to build their strength and confidence. Call it a rehearsal for real life.

Role-playing lets children experience mistakes safely at home and away from public arenas where they could be embarrassed or hurt by making mistakes in front of friends. Role-playing allows many opportunities to practice skills—like refusing peer pressure—in a protected environment. And role-playing drives home the point that other people may be manipulative or selfish while their outward actions and words hide underlying motives.

Scores of opportunities exist in daily life events, on TV, and in movies to open up role-playing occasions. The most obvious and horrendous ones are news reports of young people toting guns into schools or teenage parents dumping their newborn baby in a trash bin before returning to the high school dance. Other role-playing opportunities can begin when you see television characters being forced into situations that can result in drunkenness or date rape. Or when you drive into a parking lot where a cluster of teenagers is puffing up a gray cloud of smoke. These occasions, whether dramatic or relatively minor, may not concern your child directly, but they can be used as jumping-off points to role-play.

Here is an example of role-playing: Dad and his ten-year-old are in the car, waiting for the traffic light to turn green. At the bus stop on the corner, they notice a cluster of high school students jostling each other. One yanks another's backpack and tosses it over a fence. It looks like a fight could break out—a typical teenage scene.

Dad could ignore it, say nothing, and drive on when the light changes, or he could use it as a chance to role-play. If he seizes this opportunity, he could open a role-playing conversation like this:

"See that? I wonder what's going to happen."

"I don't know," his son answers without much interest.

"What do you suppose the kid whose backpack was taken will do next?"

The ten-year-old looks out the car window more intently. "Maybe punch out the kid. He looks pretty mad."

"What do you think that will lead to?"

"Prob'ly a fight. His friends will jump the other one's friends."

The light changes so this parent and child do not learn the outcome, but Dad continues the role-playing:

"What could the kid do instead of fighting the boy who took his backpack?"

"Call him a name or something to make everyone know he's stupid."

"But won't that just make him madder, make him have to fight so that he is not embarrassed in front of his friends?"

The boy thinks a while before replying. "Maybe wait 'til the bus comes, and after all the kids get on, he could hop over the fence, get his backpack, and make it look like he missed the bus. That way, he wouldn't look like a big wuss, and he could take the next bus."

"Yes, that's a pretty smart way to get out of a tricky situation. But what do you think would happen if a fight had broken out?"

"Never know. Somebody might have pulled a knife."

"Yeah, I like your idea better."

One of the best places to do role-playing is in the car. After all, an automobile is a lethal weapon—a child cannot jump out! Talking in the car also allows intimacy without eye contact. If the subject is awkward or embarrassing, parent and child do not have to look at each other directly. This allows something of a comfort zone so kids are less likely to clam up or feel that they are being interrogated or "taught a lesson."

Whether role-playing occurs in the car or elsewhere, it should have a light, casual tone. Do not try to drum a lesson into your child by pounding home point after point. Just move subtly from one point to the next without giving away your hidden agenda. If your child seems to get stuck at one step, try to think of another angle to approach it and get him unstuck. And try not to hopscotch over sequential steps or your message will get lost and your child will not follow along to the ultimate "Ah-Ha!"

Rules for Role-Playing

Before you begin role-playing, consider the following ground rules.

The first rule.   Look for teachable moments or occasions. Ideally, these crop up as neutral situations that involve other people, real or fictional, not your child directly. Role-plays based on external events are far more comfortable for your child to engage in than one in which a father says, for example, "OK, now I'm going to play your boyfriend, and if I ask you to come to my house after school and have sex, what will you say?" Such personalized role-playing will freak out any daughter. Her reaction most likely will be "Yuck!"

The second rule.   Never, ever tell your child that you are doing a role-play. Do not announce, "It's time for a role-play." For it to work successfully, role-playing must be subtly presented, casual and low-key. Otherwise, it will seem phony both to you and your child, who will feel self-conscious and tune you out. Simply begin with a straightforward observation or question, something along these lines: "How do you think Rachel [a TV or movie character] could have handled that situation?" or "What would happen if she did something else?"

The third rule. Avoid in-your-face role-plays that are confrontational or belligerent, such as "This is what will happen to you if you . . . " If you use hyped-up scare tactics like that, it will only raise your child's anxiety level, which is not conducive to helping him think things through step by step. Keep the tone calm, loving, encouraging, and objective.

The fourth rule. Use short, universal phrases. Let your preteen do most of the talking. Add some encouraging words such as "umm," "yeah," "I see," and "I hear you" to keep the conversational ball rolling. Keep your own "adult" language to a minimum. When adolescents hear stodgy, sophisticated, or academic words, they assume that adults do not understand their reality. If your words smack of pretension, they are likely to say, "It's not like that" or "That's corny" (which means "Shut up, old man, you are a fool") and they are no longer listening to you.

The fifth rule. Avoid using teen language. They change it every Tuesday in secret meetings. By the time you think you have caught on, I promise you, they will be speaking a new language. If you try to sound way cool, dude, they will see right through you and scoff.

The sixth rule. Stay calm and quiet to allow your children to *think* instead of react. Do not jump in with suggestions. It is not your job to fill in the blanks; it is theirs.

Now you are ready to start role-playing. Like any new skill, it may not feel comfortable or be instantly successful. Practice is required. Do not get discouraged if your child's initial reaction is "What are you doing, Mom? You don't usually talk like that." This is new for you and your child, so it may be awkward at first. But you will get the hang of it.

Practice Thinking About Alternatives

Scores of role-playing opportunities can be used to teach lessons and practice skills in safe settings. Some are real-life situations, but television offers many others, and the beauty there is that kids are already interested in the situation on the screen.

What television shows do your kids watch? Sit down with them once in a while when they are watching their favorite programs. Do not worry; you are not expected to become a regular fan. Watch ads as well as programs that are targeted especially at teens. Get up close and personal with the characters. Most mainstream TV shows are incredibly predictable, so it will not take you long to recognize various characters' traits. When a particular character is about to do something stupid, harmful, or destructive to himself or someone else, take note of it. You may even find it useful to leave the room after the show and scribble some notes that you can use for future role-playing. (Obviously do not take notes in front of your kids or they will think that you are nuts or are trying some subversive way to get inside their heads, which, by the way, you are!)

Now think like a scriptwriter. List as many other scenarios as you can. What alternative choices could the character have made? What else could he or she have said or done? How would each of the other options have changed the outcome? Watching these programs and taking notes is simply a warmup exercise—or a homework assignment—to help you practice thinking in this "what are the alternatives?" pattern. This is the pattern that you will use to guide your child to think about similar scenarios.

When you are ready to start a role-play, launch into it casually by asking about a character's action and motivations: "What do you think will happen if Steven decides to do X? What else could he do? What would have happened if he did Y instead?" Ask your child to suggest different paths a character might take to avoid or to get safely out of a negative situation. If Steven takes step A, will it more likely lead to outcome B or C? Then what could occur? Are there things that the character could have done to prevent the potentially dangerous situation from arising in the first place?

When you base role-playing on a television program, make a game of it. Have fun. Keep the tone light. If you are too serious, your child will not want to watch TV with you. Do not be so heavy-handed that your child recognizes that you are using a television program to teach a lesson. Instead, ham it up if this feels comfortable to you. Sit on the edge of your seat and pretend to be freaked out by some dangerous mistake that a character is about to make. Root for the character—as you might for your favorite athlete—to get past the hazard. Use humor or dramatic, exaggerated reactions ("Oh, my God! I can't believe it! Why did she do *that*?" you might say, slapping your forehead).

When you practice thinking about alternatives with your child, you are helping her clarify the agenda. You are showing your preteen how a small change can significantly alter an outcome; how a different answer (a firm "no" for example) can protect someone from getting into a dangerous situation; or how a kind, supportive comment to a troubled friend can help him avoid further emotional hurt.

Wrong Answers Are OK

If you and your preteen get stuck doing a role-play—say, for example, that your child cannot come up with an alternative choice or suggests one that you think is completely off-base— catch yourself from jumping in. Do not supply a solution or correct his answer. Remember, it is the step-by-step *process* that is important here, not the perfect solution. This is, after all, a hypothetical situation, a bogus "life experience" where mistakes cannot hurt your child directly.

Even when we catch ourselves launching into a lecture and stop, we sometimes fall into the pattern of supplying short answers or hints, a form of teasing out the "right" answer from our children. This is natural because we DO have more knowledge and wiser judgment than preteens. The answers seem so apparent and simple to us. But it does them no good if we supply them with ready-made answers. Young people do not learn that way. They need to find the answers for themselves, even the "wrong" answers, if the lesson is to become meaningful and real. And they feel more respected when parents recognize that they can come to their own conclusions.

If you have the tendency, which many of us have, toward giving children answers, you will probably find that it is a difficult pattern to break. One suggestion can help: Practicing with another adult before you expect to do so successfully with your preteen can help you overcome this habit. Ask your spouse or a friend to be a guinea pig. Let's say your friend is just learning a sport or hobby that you mastered years ago. Try to teach your friend without lecturing or giving him all the answers at once. Practice letting him make some mistakes. If his thing is gourmet cooking, for example, do not turn down the flame just as he is about to scorch the butter. Let him burn it so he learns just how low the flame should be. He can always clean the pan and start over.

It is OK, even desirable, for kids to make mistakes and come up with incorrect answers as long as it is done in a safe setting. So practice steering your children one step at a time toward reaching their own conclusions and solutions. Encourage them to find answers without judging the validity of their solutions. Do not say, for example, "That's a silly answer. You don't know what will happen." Let your child spin out a scenario that may seem ridiculous or stupid to you. That's good! He will see the mistake in the end when negative outcomes result, but he will have made this discovery in the safety of spinning out alternatives with you by his side.

Decision Trees

We want young people to understand and accept important, universal concepts, such as the following:

- Teen pregnancy can change the rest of your life.

- It's important to stay in school and to get a good education.

- Fighting back in retaliation can lead to deeper trouble or physical danger.

But these concepts are too vague and global for a young adolescent who is still thinking in concrete terms. If we try to paint these abstract lessons in broad strokes, they have little relevance to a child under age fourteen. We have learned we cannot teach these concepts by lecturing because that route is a dead end.

Here is another approach, a more effective way to get across important but abstract concepts: pick up a pencil and a piece of paper and sketch *a decision tree* to illustrate the clear *progression* from certain decisions to their possible outcomes. A decision tree is a very concrete way to break down a theoretical concept into realistic, step-by-step segments that a young adolescent can actually see and grasp because it shows each decision point along the path from action to outcome. It does not require any artistic talent, but once you diagram a basic decision tree, you and your child can repeat the exercise by using various circumstances and dilemmas. Decision trees can be used to illustrate both wise and unwise ideas and decisions.

Let's take a look at how one of the broad concepts above could be sketched as a decision tree. Here is the background: A fourteen-year-old is frustrated by schoolwork and fearful about entering high school next September. He explodes, "I hate school. It's dumb. The teachers are stupid. I'm going to drop out as soon as I can and get a job."

A typical parent's response would be similar to this: "No, you won't. That would ruin your life. As long as you're living in this house, you'll stay in school. I've been breaking my back to save some money every year for your college education. No way are you going to be a high school dropout! Don't you understand that you'll have no opportunities without an education? What do you want to do with the rest of your life, flip burgers 'til you retire?"

"Blah, blah, blah" is all the child hears by this point. "Wha wa . . . Wha wa . . . Wha wa . . ."

In place of the typical response, the parent could substitute, "Umm. I think that might be making a mistake. Let's think

Decision Trees

All right, you drop out of school and you get a job. How much do you think you'll make an hour now? When do you think you'll get a raise? How much?

↓

It's five years from now and you are ready to start a family and want to move out. How much are you making a year?

↓

OK, pay rent. How much is that?

↓

OK, pay for your children's clothes and food. How much do you have left?

↓

Go ahead. Try to get a higher-paying job. Anything standing in your way?

↓

When your child wants help with his algebra homework how will you handle that? When your child says that he doesn't need to finish school because you didn't, how do you handle that?

All right, let's try the other option. Let's say you finish school. (By the way, what can we do to make this easier for you? Tutoring, homework help?) You get a job with a (high school/college) diploma. How much do you make now?

about this and see what might happen." Then Mom or Dad could sketch a decision tree and ask the child's input when questions arise.

Before you pick up a pencil and paper to sketch a decision tree with your child, I suggest you practice on your own once or twice. Why not start with a tough one? For example: "Teen pregnancy can change your whole life." How would you use the decision tree format to break down that broad concept into small steps leading to and supporting that conclusion?

After you have practiced sketching a few decision trees and are ready to use the format with your child, remember to guide your child with specific, detailed questions. Remember: do not supply the answers or solutions. And—perhaps most important—do not worry if your child gives the "wrong" answer or makes what you believe is a bad decision. That is the beauty of this exercise: *it is just an exercise.*

When a child makes a wrongheaded choice on a decision tree, she will see where it leads. She can retrace her steps, scratch out a poor choice, reconsider, and take alternate routes. Let's hope our kids *do* make some mistakes with a decision tree, in fact. It is safer when they do so on a piece of paper and in our presence than out in the real world.

As effective as decision trees can be, I would also caution against overusing them. If you whip out your pencil and start to sketch one too often, your children will see that you have an agenda. It will seem too much like school. Use this technique only when it feels comfortable and appropriate.

Decision trees should be reserved for momentous occasions when a child is facing a significant problem. Don't assume that you should sketch one for everyday conflicts. Save the decision tree technique for the major issues.

Here is one other caution. We adults can lay out very concretely all the likely outcomes of particular decisions. To us—and to most kids—the decision tree makes the various consequences absolutely clear. (Take teen pregnancy as an example. A decision tree could show how having a baby during adolescence will lead to fewer educational opportunities and lower-paying jobs. It will raise questions like "Who's going to pay for the diapers? Who's going to take care of the baby when you want to go out?" and so forth.)

Yet as glaringly obvious as those outcomes appear to us, they may not make a difference to the young person who desires instant gratification. If that happens, you may want to consider whether self-esteem problems, depression, or hopelessness (specifically a lack of caring about the future) might be at the root of the child's inability to grasp future consequences. In that case, a decision tree is simply not adequate. Really listen for the underlying motivations that may be driving the child's need for what you consider undesirable behavior. You may want to seek an evaluation by a health care professional.

Although decision trees are meant for the Big Issues, also keep in mind that they can be used occasionally in situations where the outcome may not necessarily be dire. Here is an example of how one mother used a decision tree to point toward a constructive future:

In late spring, Rachel began talking about her summer plans. She thought she might just hang out with friends all summer long. Maybe she would grow bored, but she didn't have any other ideas. Her mom did not believe that twelve weeks of totally free time would be such a great idea, so she used a decision tree.

"Let's take a look at this, Rachel, " she began, as she took the calendar off the wall and a pen and paper from the desk drawer. "Now, after school ends, there will be three weeks in June, four weeks in July, and five weeks in August. Let's think of what could happen over the summer . . . "

With Rachel's input, they sketched several possibilities. On the downside, she couldn't hang out with her best friend because she was going to a sleepover camp for eight weeks; two other friends were going on vacation with their families for a few weeks. And even though Rachel had been invited to spend a week with out-of-state cousins, a lot of empty time would be left over. On the other hand, if she found something interesting to do—at this point Rachel herself suggested volunteering at a neighborhood daycare center—then she would be less bored and still have free time in the late afternoons and evenings to spend with friends.

Her mother added that working with young children might not only be fun, but also it could have long-term advantages. Rachel's mother drew several boxes representing college and career possibilities.

"Since you've always been great with little kids and have sometimes said you might like to become a teacher," she pointed out, "this summer experience might be good background for college and later a teaching job." And as she spoke those words, she drew lines on the decision tree leading from the daycare box to those future possibilities. Then Rachel added a few more: "Yeah, let's draw a line for next summer. Maybe then I could get a paid job working with kids if I volunteer at daycare this summer, and maybe I'll meet some parents who will hire me to babysit."

Choreographed Discussions

A *choreographed discussion* is a fancy term for just talking. But the difference between a choreographed discussion and a casual, spontaneous conversation with your child is that *you have an agenda* when you initiate a choreographed discussion. You can use a choreographed discussion as a teaching tool to guide your child toward a realization that will enhance his safety, assure his success in handling a challenge, or increase his sense of responsibility. It is similar to dancing. You know the steps. They are well thought out, but they may take your audience by surprise. They are, of course, best when they look spontaneous and unrehearsed, but essentially they are decision trees in the air.

Before I give you an example of a choreographed discussion, here are some basic guidelines:

- Listen; do not lecture and do not interrupt.

- Split the broad concept into several smaller parts. Picture a road map of where you are headed in your mind and plan on making several stops along the way.

- At each stop, make certain that your child has grasped the intended idea before moving ahead. If you are unsure about whether he has grasped the point, go back a few steps before moving forward. Do not expect quick or immediate success. It could take days or several conversations to travel along this route. (And it is OK to get sidetracked or detoured! Sometimes those meandering back roads produce great, serendipitous conversations between parent and child.)

- Talk as little as possible; guide your child to come up with as many answers on his own as he possibly can.

The issue in this example is drug prevention for preteens and early adolescents. The image of children using drugs terrifies most parents, so they try a preemptive strike to scare kids away from drugs. How? Typically, they launch into a lecture: "I don't want you to try drugs—ever! If I catch you with drugs, I'll punish you like you've never been punished before. Drug dealers are evil people who want to harm you, to get you hooked. You'll ruin your life, maybe end up dead."

There are several problems with this approach. Lectures turn kids off. Preteens and young teens generally do not get into drugs to rebel or to medicate emotional problems, as older adolescents tend to do. Younger kids usually just want to try something that older kids do. And as we learned in Chapter 2, preteens are not very savvy about other people's motivations because they still think in terms of good and bad. If we try to frighten a child by portraying drug dealers as bad people, that tactic may backfire because the concrete-thinking preteen may be prepared to meet the "evil" drug dealers but unprepared to deal with real-life situations. When an older teen or an adult drug dealer approaches a preteen, the ususal pitch goes like this:

"Hey, little buddy! You're one of the eighth graders, right?"

"No. I'm in fifth grade."

"No kidding? You look a lot older. I just thought you were hanging out with younger kids. You want to try some of this? Or maybe you're not really old enough yet."

"I am so!"

"OK, you seem pretty cool. I'll let you have some of my stash for free." The child is flattered. He thinks this older person is nice to offer him something for free.

Consider how the following choreographed conversation can be far more effective than a lecture to prepare your child for an all-to-real situation.

PARENT: "Suppose some guys offered you drugs. Do you think they would be nice or mean?"

PRETEEN: "Probably mean."

PARENT: "I'm not sure. They might be nice. What if they gave you drugs for free? Why do you think they'd do that?"

PRETEEN: "Maybe because they liked me or wanted to be friendly."

PARENT: "Maybe, but I don't know. Let's think about this for a minute . . . You know how the grocery store gives out coupons? Why do you think the grocer does that?"

PRETEEN: "'Cause he likes his customers and wants to help them save money."

PARENT: "Suppose he gives out coupons for cereal. You want me to buy it?"

PRETEEN: "Yeah, if I like that kind."

PARENT: "So I buy the cereal a few times because you like it. But what if the store stops handing out the coupons? You want me to keep buying that cereal?"

PRETEEN: "Yeah."

PARENT: "Why do you think the grocery store owner started giving out those coupons in the first place?"

PRETEEN: "Oh, so we'll try that cereal and keep buying it and he'll make money."

PARENT: "Right. Now, what about a drug dealer who offers you drugs for free? Is he doing it to be a nice guy, just to be friendly?"

PRETEEN: "Oh, yeah! I get it. So I'll want more and even pay for it!"

This child has clearly come to his own cognitive Ah-Ha because the parent guided him skillfully and subtly through this series of small, concrete steps to reach his own conclusion. Now he is ready to hear about how drug dealers portray themselves as kind people just trying to offer kids a good time.

Choreographed conversations are used most dramatically when there is a major issue or situation at hand, like a child's declaration that he wants to drop out of school. But because they can fit naturally into conversation, they may become your most often used skill. You will find that you can swing into choreographed conversations subtly for less dramatic situations. You know the direction you want to take your child; you will initiate a conversation casually; you will listen to be sure your child is following your line of thought and, if not, you will take a few steps back to be sure he or she catches up. The more you use choreographed conversations, the more at ease you and your child will become with this most effective, easily digestible method of guidance.

Pulling It Together

Role-plays, decision trees, and choreographed conversations have several things in common. They get young people to think through a scenario under safe guidance. They offer them a means to become aware of a problem, consider consequences, and therefore become motivated to avoid the problem. Each technique offers a young adolescent the opportunity to build skills or to think through a situation step by step.

Communication with young people should be mostly unstructured. I am not suggesting that every time you talk with your child you should follow an agenda or communicate with a special, prescribed technique. Rather, continue to have a natural, easygoing relationship. But when you have to make a point, be sure you are well-equipped to make it effectively. Don't alienate your son or daughter by lecturing in the traditional fashion. Practice these alternative techniques to make sure you become comfortable enough with them that they can flow as smoothly as possible. In short, you can learn to *lecture without lecturing* by using the ability to draw from these different techniques effortlessly. Much of the time, you will be able to use a mixture of the three techniques: role-plays, choreographed discussions, and decision trees.

Here is an example from my own medical practice. It is a frightening situation, and one that I hope you and your children never face, but I offer it to show how these techniques can work with even the most dramatic challenges and to illustrate how they can readily be combined:

A fourteen-year-old girl, whom I will call Lydia, came to my office because her eye had been injured in a fight with a classmate. Her injury was minor. The medical treatment was simple. But I could not let her leave my office without first making sure that she was not in immediate danger of further injury and without trying to guide her toward a better understanding of the dangers of confrontation. I started by asking her some nonjudgmental questions.

I asked her what made her angry enough to fight. This is a great question to assess whether someone has a low or high threshold for fighting. All kids seem to have basic rules for fighting: First, they insult the intended victim with words. If that fails, they insult the person's family. If that does not work, they "step up to them" or "get in their face" by invading their body space. Finally, they push the victim. When I ask a young person what makes him mad enough to fight, the answer tells me a lot about his anger threshold and what I need to do to help guide him to be safe.

Lydia said the fight was triggered by the other girl's insults about her clothes, but what really made her angry enough to fight was the girl's derogatory comments about Lydia's mother.

"Is the fight over? What do you plan to do when you see this girl again?" I asked her.

"Kill her. That's why I got this knife." She pulled it out of her pocket and showed it to me proudly.

When a teenager talks openly about contemplating such a violent act, an adult's natural reaction would be to shout, "Don't do that, you idiot! You will ruin your life. You'll go to jail." Yet such a response would seem to Lydia like any other adult's attempt to control her life. A lecture would be pointless. She would not hear it. Even if we confiscated the knife, she could easily replace it.

I read Lydia's boast to kill the girl as a plea for help. She knew that by showing me the knife, I would keep her from using it. So my challenge was to convince her to scrap her plan by making her realize the lifelong consequences of such a violent act—all without alienating her. I could not simply tell her that her plan was dangerous and wrong. I had to lead her to reach those conclusions herself. The "lecture" was clear: "Don't you realize that the action you are taking today will destroy your life? You will be kicked out of school and never finish your education. You will go to jail. Your mother will be disgraced.

You will have no kids, no good job. And when you are older and finally out of jail, you will have no family." Had I taken this lecture route, she would have heard *Wha Wha Wha* and become angry with me for telling her what to do when I could not possibly understand her life.

"Let's think about this," I said as I began a choreographed conversation. "What do you want to happen when you go to school today?"

"I want her to die."

I suggested to Lydia that I would like to think through the possibilities of what could happen that day. I started a very calm role-play as I wrote down the results of what we were learning through the role-play on a decision tree. Then I asked her to take out her comb and "stab" me—very slowly—in the arm. As she began, I grabbed her comb and—also in very slow motion—pretended to stab her in the back with it.

"If this had been real, you would be what is called 'maimed.' You know what that means?" I asked.

"Yeah, maybe in a wheelchair, like paralyzed. There's a man on my street like that." I listened as she recalled the victims of violence in her neighborhood.

"Right. If somebody gets stabbed in the spine, she could be in pain all the time or never able to walk again. Did you ever think about that possibility?"

"No."

I paused as she realized, perhaps for the first time, that she could become a victim herself.

"Let's try it again," I suggested. This time I pretended to stab her in the heart with the comb.

"If the other girl stabbed you in the heart, what would that mean?"

"I'd be dead."

Mapping Out the Long-Range Consequences

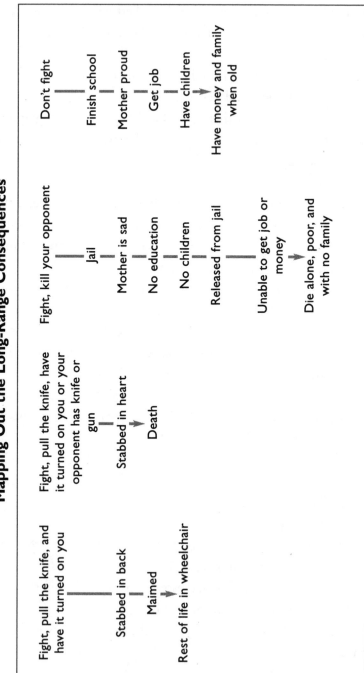

"Right. Have you thought about ending up dead today when you put that knife in your pocket?"

She said she had not, but I did not want to end the lesson there.

"Let's see what could happen if she hadn't grabbed your knife and turned on you. What if you actually did stab and kill her? How would that make you feel?"

"Good."

"For how long would you feel good?"

"All day."

"What happens the next day?" I asked.

"I get probation?"

I explained briefly (and in a matter-of-fact tone) that first-degree murder would be the likely charge because she had come to school equipped with a lethal weapon. She probably would be tried as an adult and sentenced to thirty years in jail. Then I added, "By the way, how would your mom feel?"

"I guess she feels pretty sad because I'm not going to be home any more."

I then started to sketch a decision tree that led Lydia through a scenario where she would never finish school, get a job, or have a family of her own. And she would live and die alone after her prison release. I wrote down each step as I guided her both to come up with an answer and to contemplate its impact. I did little talking and mostly listened. Then I asked, "Suppose you let this girl live. How would you feel?"

"Bad."

"How long would you feel bad?"

"All day."

Score! The cognitive "Ah-Ha!" switched on. The light bulb lit up! Suddenly Lydia realized *herself* that it was foolish to risk her whole life to feel good for just one day. Take a look at the decision tree on page 82 that we developed in our choreographed discussion and acted out through a very calm role-play.

Two lives saved! Brilliant, isn't it? No, not brilliant at all. It is really very simple. If you believe it is brilliant, you may worry about your own ability to do this. It was just a lecture filled with reason, but delivered in small concrete steps that allowed the teenager to figure it all out herself.

Modeling

As much as we consciously guide our children by role-playing, decision trees, and choreographed conversations, we may overlook another essential way to teach awareness and support appropriate behavior. That is through the expression of our own attitudes, values, relationships, and actions. Usually we do not model behavior with much premeditation, but we should remind ourselves from time to time that we are significant models for our children.

Kids watch us closely. We generally are not aware of it, and they certainly try not to get caught eyeing us—that would be entirely uncool. But they *do* observe our actions, expressions, and decisions. They hear our words. So it is important to be aware that we are modeling behavior all the time. For example, integrity is one of the qualities that young people value most. If we preach one thing (like "Don't swear") and do the opposite (like cursing at drivers on the highway), kids' antennae shoot up and we are seen as hypocrites. And you can be sure that the next time you catch them swearing, they will remind you, "But I heard you say that, too."

I am not suggesting that parents must behave perfectly at every moment—of course, that is completely unrealistic. But we are their models in good times and bad. When we are under stress or facing a crisis, it is important to show them how we handle it. We can model emotional intelligence for them. By talking openly about the situation, we can show them that we try to think calmly before a problem gets ugly, figure out the consequences, and choose the best options before we act.

Young teenagers would be offended if we told them how or what to think, but there is no reason why we cannot let them in on *our* thinking process—how we plan, problem-solve, or organize our thoughts. After a difficult day at work, we could mention a problem and how we reacted: "My coworker was really slacking off, and I knew extra work would pile up for me, so I thought about what I could say to him before it got worse." You do not have to launch into lengthy scripts, but simply drop a few comments such as "To handle this problem, I think I will . . . or maybe I could . . . " or "When I am in a situation like this, I ask myself questions like, 'What will happen tomorrow or how big a deal will this seem like next week?'" or "You know, this would have turned out better if I had chosen to do X instead of Y." If we have screwed up or hurt someone, we can also present a model, such as "I blew that one. I am really sorry."

You also could spell out a minor dilemma and invite your child to suggest solutions: "This problem at work really bugs me, and I'm not sure what I should do. What would you do?" Obviously, these examples should be scaled to your child's age and abilities. I would not expect you to seek input from a ten-year-old on the pros and cons of a major business deal. But you can sketch out dilemmas that preteens understand. You will probably be astonished at some of their suggestions. You also may be surprised at how interested they are in you and your work life. And though they will not tell you, they do appreciate your asking for their input. It makes them feel grown-up, trusted, and respected.

The point to remember is *model a thinking process*. Demonstrate how to look at a problem from various angles, consider several possible outcomes, and make the best decision. You can, in effect, give your children a road map for similar situations that they will run into in the future. And even when we do not make the smartest decisions, we can show them that we pick ourselves up and start all over again.

When It Seems Almost Impossible

I would like to conclude this chapter on a high note, but the simple fact is that our good intentions and well-honed skills will sometimes fail. We can draw the clearest decision tree, win an Oscar for Best Role-Player, craft the best choreographed conversation, and model the most exemplary behavior, but children on occasion will reject our guidance or get in over their heads. I hope that does not happen often, but when it does there is something you can do. It has happened to me with some of my most challenging patients. When a caring adult cannot help a young person think through a difficult situation, it is often because the adolescent has become so hopeless that he concludes he has no control at all. Without a sense of control, young people do not believe they can change.

When none of the above strategies works, I tell a young person, "I know you are in trouble, but I do not know the right

Teens Know Which Ladder to Choose

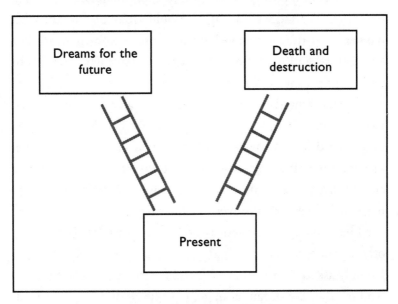

thing to say. I don't have the answer for you. It's up to you to figure it out. Let's see what could happen."

Then I pull out a pencil and sheet of paper. I draw two ladders and explain that each represents two possible roads the child can travel. Both ladders begin in the present, but each leads to a different but plausible outcome. One ends in serious trouble or even death. The other leads to the child's dream, such as college, a satisfying job, a family, or however he or she describes it.

I try to make the challenge less overwhelming by explaining that all one has to do is take the first step in a positive direction to get on the right road. I ask them only to figure out that first step. This can be very difficult and require some prompting. But once they do come up with a first step, they realize that "one step at a time" is a manageable way to achieve some control.

Sometimes, though, they cannot even imagine taking that first step. The ladder leading to trouble may be fraught with dangers that they can envision but cannot seem to avoid. For example, when I used this technique with a girl who was caught up in a gang, she could not imagine how to get away from the gang's stranglehold on her life. She knew—all too realistically—that the end of that ladder would likely be physical injury, prison, or death. At the top of her "dream" ladder was her goal of becoming an architect who would create safe buildings for city children. She could not envision any way to climb off the negative ladder and take even the first step on her dream ladder.

I had no answer for getting away from the gang. But I could offer her one small opportunity to take some control in her life. I simply asked her to come back and see me the following week. And she did. We began talking about the ladders again. She still had no clear solution for getting off one ladder and onto the other. She seemed resolutely discouraged and was worried that she had disappointed me.

"But you came back today," I said, pointing at the first rung on the dream ladder. "You have just taken the first step by coming in today. You do have some control over what you do. If you didn't believe in yourself, you never would have come back to see me today." A parent can make the same point with a child who just keeps trying and remains open to your working with her to solve a problem.

She broke into tears. It really was an epiphany for her. She realized that she did have some control over her life and her choices. She was stronger and more capable than she had thought. Immediately, as she realized that she had some control, the idea to move her to the next rung on the ladder poured out. She recognized that she needed to engage her mother more in her life. She had left her hard-working mother unaware of her gang problems. Now she realized, if she confided in her mother, Mom would be able to help.

Over time, she took more steps along the constructive ladder. She attended school more regularly and spent less time with the gang. She has not yet become an architect, but she did leave the gang, finished high school, and still returns to see me from time to time. I am amazed at her resiliency. Her experience is a dramatic extreme that I hope your child will never encounter. But it serves to show that solutions to even the greatest challenges start with one small step.

Another way that adolescents often express the sense that they lack control is with a statement that goes something like this: "You keep telling me how to avoid trouble, but I have to tell you that you just don't understand. Because when your time comes, your time comes, so I might as well have fun now." I respond with a very heartfelt choreographed conversation like this:

"You know, you're right. You can't know when bad things are going to happen."

"Uh, huh, that's why I want to live while I'm young."

"I hear you," I'll say. "You know, I want to be around for a long time. But I know that I could cross the street and get hit by a bus."

"That's what I'm saying!"

"I know that I could walk across some field and get struck by lightning, or I could get caught in a drive-by shooting."

"Now you understand what I mean."

"Yeah, but you know, when I walk across a field in a lightning storm, I don't carry a big old metal pipe. When I come up to a street, I look both ways. And if a bus is barreling down the road, I don't step off the curb. And you know something else? Because I don't hang on the corners with the drug dealers, I probably won't get caught in a drive-by."

Even the most hopeless kids are often brought to tears when this choreographed conversation brings them to the realization that life is not as difficult to control as they had thought. Life is not predictable, but the excuse of having no control over it is not acceptable.

5

Skills for Dealing with Peer Pressure

Most parents tell me that their primary goal is to see their children safely through adolescence to the other side, the safe shore of adulthood across the dangerous shoals of adolescence. Their greatest fears concern the risky behaviors that could pull their teenagers under, the pitfalls and perils of adolescence that many parents feel are beyond their ability to prevent or protect from. This chapter is about survival skills—skills to teach and reinforce so our kids will land safely on the other shore.

In the last chapter we discussed techniques to help children realize that there are consequences to behaviors—without using the classic but ineffective and alienating lecture method. Making young adolescents aware of potential consequences is a vital first step because no child can make a safe decision if she does not first know that a problem exists. But that's only part of it.

She may be motivated to steer clear of a problem, but she may not know *how* to avoid it.

The Necessity of Survival Skills

Let's take this to the next level. Your child has become aware that a problem or potential problem exists. You promoted that awareness either by presenting specific brief facts or by guiding him to his own recognition of consequences with the techniques (decision trees, choreographed discussions, modeling) spelled out previously. Now your child wants to change. He is motivated. But what happens if he does not know *how* to make the change? You might as well push him out into a stormy sea in a rowboat without oars. He needs the skills—the tools and equipment—to make the desired changes.

Unfortunately most young teenagers lack survival skills. Adults have not taught and practiced them with their children. This deficiency is made worse by timing. It is precisely at this moment when peer pressure kicks in like a tornado. Young teens who lack survival skills are particularly vulnerable to negative peer pressure.

Remember that this is the dawning of the independence spurt. "I don't need you any more, Mom and Dad. I'm going to be my own person, an individual," they are starting to think and say.

In reality, that translates to "I'm going to be an individual—*just like all my friends.*"

If you do not believe that, stroll down the corridor of any middle school or junior high. How similar are the clothes, hairstyles, vocabulary, and even the body language? When teenagers announce that they want to be individuals, they usually mean that they want to be different from their parents, not their friends. As frustrating as that might be, it is developmentally normal.

The adolescent need to fit in with the crowd, to be accepted by this *new family* of peers, is paramount at the very moment that each child wants to be an individual. Even young people who *don't* look like the majority of other kids are striving to fit in by looking just the opposite. The few who dress completely in black or wear trench coats like a uniform are making a choice about joining a peer group. They are stating, "I don't want to look like all those preppy kids. I'm an outsider. I'm different. I'm an individual." But they, too, are trying to express their emerging individuality by identifying with a different, though numerically smaller, group of peers.

This need to fit in explains peer pressure better than those frightening After School Specials you may remember. Only a fraction of peer pressure is the classic "I'm going to force you to do something I want you to do" type. Peer pressure is generally much more subtle. It is more internally driven and motivated by a young person's desire to fit in. He so wishes to be accepted that the group's action takes on a life of its own and influences his behavior even though no group member actually tells him what to do. For this reason, the most effective ways to protect children from negative peer pressure are by making sure that your child belongs to a positive peer group, promoting good self-esteem, and teaching positive strategies to deal with life's stresses. All the same, the kind of harmful interactions so often labeled "peer pressure" certainly do exist, and there is no excuse for not preparing your child to deal with them.

The Gift of Skills

The remainder of this chapter will describe specific survival skills that you can teach your children to help them resist negative peer pressure. These skills can help them maintain the values you have taught them and refuse peer pressure to try risky behaviors. But before we get into the details, let's consider some basic ground rules. If you master these at the beginning, your skill-teaching will go more smoothly.

1. Keep the tone casual. As suggested earlier when I explained role-playing, do not broadcast what you are doing. Do not tell children that you are doing a role-play or teaching them a survival skill. They will only respond by seeing you as Mommy or Daddy Dork. Instead, launch these skill sessions as spontaneously as you can by opening with a statement like "Well, what would you say if . . . "

2. Do not try to be cool. Also as you do when role-playing, avoid teen lingo, especially because their "in" terms change every week. If you attempt to use teenage slang, your kids will see right through it. And if you use the wrong term or an outdated one, they will undoubtedly respond with something along the lines of "Where'd you get that one? It's not like that!" This translates as "What do you know? You were never my age." And that takes the focus off your message. So substitute short, universal phrases for teenage slang. And let your child do most of the talking.

3. Avoid in-your-face fear tactics. If you are trying to teach a survival skill that will help your child out of a potentially dangerous situation, such as getting out of a party where everyone is stoned or drunk, do not overplay your hand with end-of-the-world scenarios. This can lead you into a tirade about date rape, police raids, and other frightening possibilities. No shouting in their faces, "Do you know what would happen in prison?"

If you use scare tactics, you will be prompting your child to react, not think about it calmly. The focus will either be on the hyped-up scare ("Ohmygod! That would really be trouble!") or on your overreaching ("Ohmygod! That'll never happen. Dad's just trying to frighten me."). Either way, the child is reacting emotionally only, rather than thinking the situation through. Scare tactics also increase a child's stress, as we'll discuss in the next chapter, and they can backfire by pushing a child in a destructive direction to cope with that stress.

4. Always be on the lookout for opportunities to teach skills. Try to develop a habit of finding naturally occurring occasions or events that do not directly involve your child—like the street corner scene mentioned earlier (page 62). These openings pop up more often than you might expect if you put out your antennae to notice them. Television offers plenty of opportunities showing people making mistakes. A simple comment like, "Now she could have handled that differently, don't you think?" can open up a discussion with your child about *how* a fictional character might have made other choices or taken different actions to get a more positive outcome or avoid trouble. Real-life events—dinner table conversations about kids at school or adults you know or work with, as well as news reports—also provide a cornucopia of opportunities to teach skills. When you see a report on the local news about police arresting drug dealers across town, you could open a dialogue with a simple question like, "How do you think they get kids your age to try drugs?"

Comments about fictional or real events affecting other people allow you to open on neutral ground. Since your child is not personally involved, he does not feel defensive. You are not conducting an inquisition (as you would if you said something like, "Do your friends use drugs? Did anyone ever try to sell you drugs?"), so a child is more comfortable engaging in a conversation with you.

Now, on to the actual survival skills. They fall into three categories of refusing negative peer pressure: saying "no," reversing the pressure or responding to lines, and shifting the blame to parents.

"Just Say No"

In the 1980s Nancy Reagan took a lot of grief for her antidrug slogan "Just Say No." Critics thought the advice was oversimplified, even naive. Comedians poked fun at it on late night television. While the slogan certainly did not stop teenage drug use, the concept behind it does have value.

The word *no* can be very powerful, but it has to be used correctly—and sparingly—to be effective. Listen to adults in a supermarket, for example: A toddler is begging for candy at the check-out counter.

"No candy. We'll eat dinner as soon as we get home," says the exhausted, impatient parent.

The child begs, whines, verges on a tantrum.

"I said 'no,' OK?" the parent responds.

The bored, tired, hungry child does not hear the *no*. She hears the "*OK*?" so she will not give in easily. "Hmmmm," she thinks, "Mommy said no, but she's asking me if it's OK. No, it's not OK. I want that candy."

Well, we know how this story ends. I have seen many parents in situations like this. Sometimes they say *no* when they actually mean: "This is what I know I should say, but my heart really isn't in it. So go ahead, push me and you'll get what you want." That may be why so many parental statements end with the question "OK?"

I am a strong believer in "the gift of few *no*s." If you have spent the last decade telling your children *no* with every third breath, the word probably has little impact. And even if it has impact, chances are that your child is complying out of rote reaction. On the other hand, if you can develop a habit of uttering as few *no*s as possible, you are giving your children a double gift. One gift is the opportunity for them to be creative. With few *no*s in their lives, they are freer to explore the world actively. The second part of the gift comes from the old more-is-less axiom: When you do use *no* sparingly, your children know that you really mean it. The less often it is spoken, the more powerful it becomes when you must use it for serious issues.

Another *no* problem: Many parents say *no* with a smile or with body language that implies *yes* or *maybe*. Or they say it without any steel in their voices. I'm certainly not advocating authoritarian parenting or advising you to shout "No!" with fire and brimstone, but I do think that parents need to consider how and when they say *no*.

What kind of lesson do children learn over the first decade of life if their parents have been modeling this No–Maybe–Well, OK standard? By the time they reach early adolescence, these kids have absorbed a harmful lesson: "*No* does not always mean *no*." They have been receiving mixed signals. The word *no* holds little or no power for them. And that can be dangerous in adolescence. The power of the word *no* is a great example, in fact, of how a parent's modeling can be more important than any special communication technique. Use *no* sparingly, but when you do say it, mean it. And say it with clarity. Your children may resent those *no*s, but they will learn from your example either to discount the power of the word or to respect it.

Think about how the discomfort with or misunderstanding of the word *no* can be particularly dangerous in sexual situations. Though the dynamic between the sexes is certainly changing, there still is an age-old game that plays out between them. Many young women are trained and conditioned by parents, religious authorities, and/or society at large to believe that they will be considered cheap if they have sex. Young men are conditioned to believe that they should be aggressive in their pursuit of sexual relations. So let's see how these two factors play out: Boy meets girl, finds her attractive, and starts to make his moves. Girl is attracted to him. She says *no*—but with a signal. That signal might be a smile, a giggle, or some body language that sends the message "ask again" or "say the right words."

Her *no* starts to sound like *maybe*. He does not accept it as her real reply, so this mixed signal can be a setup for date rape or, at the very least, a dangerous situation. Unfortunately, most girls—even today—have learned *not* to say *no* to other people because "it sounds mean," as they often explain it. Too often girls are conditioned to be nice, agreeable, pleasant, nonconfrontational. This conditioning must be reversed.

It is quite clear: we must teach both young women and young men to understand that *no* means *no* regardless of how it is stated. Girls must learn to say *no* with conviction and without conflicting double messages. Boys must learn that *no* means *no*—no matter how it is expressed. They must understand that they are legally and morally responsible to honor that *no*. And if a young woman is under the influence of alcohol or drugs, even a *yes* equals *no*.

Though we have used sexual negotiation to illustrate this point, the power of the concept of a clear, strong *no* extends to other areas as well. During adolescence it is certainly a useful concept for any situation when a teenager might not want to engage in other negative behaviors including drug use, truancy, stealing, or violence. The truth is, if we make our preteens and early adolescents confident and comfortable with the word *no*, it will help them throughout their adult lives when colleagues and others could take advantage of them.

A key point to remember: we are not teaching them to shout *no* in a juvenile way, but to say it with clarity and firmness so that it is absolutely nonnegotiable.

How Would You Handle This Situation?

Dad and his daughter Tiffany are watching a television program when a young character is being pressured into having sex with her boyfriend.

Dad turns to Tiffany and asks, "How would you handle that?"

Tiffany answers with a slight smile, and her voice is full of embarrassment, "I would say 'No' to him."

Would you accept Tiffany's answer and let it go at that?

Don't. Do not let her off the hook with an answer she thinks *you* want to hear, an answer that will get you off her back. This is an opportunity to role-play, so make the most of it (without, of course, telling her that you're role-playing). Here is how Tiffany's father can turn this occasion into a skill-building experience:

"I saw that smile, Tiffany," he says in a light, nonaccusatory tone. "I do not believe that *no* if it comes with a smile. Let's hear it again."

"OK, Daddy. No."

"Come on, if I were that guy, I'd think you didn't mean it. Say it so it's believable."

"Oh, Daddy, you're so corny," she says (to relieve her embarrassment, but she really thinks he's pretty cool). "All right, NO." *Now* Tiffany's voice is firm. Her smile is gone.

"That's more like it. That *no* ended in an exclamation point. That's a strong, nonnegotiable *No.*"

"NO! NO!" Tiffany is now into this exercise and seems to enjoy it.

"Way to go. Now I hear that *no* loud and clear."

When you launch role-play exercises like this—whether you are teaching your child to say *no* and mean it, or any other skill—remember that it does not always go perfectly or as you might have planned. Do not be discouraged or give up. Your kids may recognize that you are trying something new (especially if you have been uttering wishy-washy *no*s for years), so they may be resistant or skeptical at first. But keep trying. Look for those small, daily opportunities to open up a role-play exercise. And even when you have carried out a successful one, repeat it from time to time. Kids this age need lots of reinforcement. We cannot assume that one good lesson will guarantee permanent protection. Think of it as lathering on sun block when you are at the beach: it washes off, so you need to reapply it on an ongoing basis.

Responding to Lines

We hear lines all the time: The garage mechanic has one to explain why he has not finished working on your car. The telemarketer has plenty of lines when she calls in the middle of dinner. Every advertisement in the media pitches a line: You'll feel younger, look better, with our product . . . You can't live without this . . . Call now!

We adults are used to lines. We recognize them for what they are: excuses for failures and mistakes or sales pitches to convince and persuade us. We know that a line tempts us with words we would like to hear, flattering phrases, something that makes us feel better. Adults also recognize that there is an ulterior motive behind every line. The person using a line is trying to put something over on us or wants to get something from us.

Most kids do not make those distinctions. They tend to accept a line at its face value the first time they hear it. They do not question the person uttering the line, and they have not yet learned to figure out what his or her underlying motivations could be. After being burned by lines, kids do recognize them. As we've said, we do not want our children to learn through hurtful mistakes, but we can speed up their learning process and minimize the dangers of real-life mistakes.

Peers use lines to exert pressure on our kids to engage in sex, to experiment with drugs, or to try other risky behaviors. To resist that pressure successfully, young teens need to be taught survival skills through role-playing or choreographed conversations. As we have seen with other exercises, these can begin with examples or scenarios from television, movies, books, or real life.

Our goal—as cynical as it may be—is to show our children how manipulative some people can be and how to respond to that manipulation. We need to teach them how to recognize a line; how to recognize the underlying motivations behind the line; and how to respond to lines in a manner that allows for no negotiation. A useful way to begin showing kids how to recognize a line is to comment about any television ad: "What a line! That's ridiculous! What do you think they want out of you?"

Then you can move on to comment about a character in a film or television program that depicts potentially harmful situations: "Why do you think he told her that? Do you think she should believe him? Will she fall for that line?"

Unlike role-playing where you do not announce to your child that you are role-playing, it is fine to talk about lines openly: "She's feeding her parents a line so they won't know she's going to that party" or "He is just flattering her so she'll fall for him. That's the oldest line in the book!"

Remember, you are teaching your children indirectly by discussing other people's use of—and response to—a line. By not commenting on your own children's behavior, you are not putting them under the spotlight. They do not feel defensive or guilty, so they are more open to learning. Many kids are actually fascinated by these discussions because it has not dawned on them yet that lines could be used so blatantly to manipulate other people. They are captivated by this new insight into teenage and adult behaviors.

Lines to Look For

Once you have introduced the broad concept of lines with your children, you can start to talk about how teenagers use lines on each other. An example of a typical teenage line begins: "I love you, and when people love each other, they . . . "

A normal teenage response would be: "I love you, too" (I've been wishing and waiting for someone I love, he or she thinks), "but it's just that I'm not ready."

That response is a sure bet—this teenager *will* have sex.

A better option is to teach your young teen to say *immediately*, "This is not about love." And make certain that you hear the period at the end of that sentence.

Rule to remember: responses should be immediate, clear, and allow no room for negotiation. They should end in a period, not a question mark.

It is a great accomplishment whenever a young person learns to recognize a line for what it is and can resist it with a strong response. But our expectations have to be realistic. Sometimes when refusal skills are taught in schools and youth groups, adults forget how difficult it is for a young person to say *no* firmly and unequivocally to friends and classmates. Developmentally many young teenagers simply do not have the strength to stand up and take an unpopular stand. Remember, they want to be accepted and popular. So if we are going to teach refusal skills effectively, we need to recognize how difficult it is for pre-teens to disagree with peers and just walk away. They may want to remain on friendly terms. They do not want to be seen as a goody-goody. They want to give their friends a way out and save face themselves.

Refusal skills, as taught in schools, typically tell adolescents to reverse the pressure. They instruct them to listen for a line and then to go right back at the other person with equal, but opposite pressure, like this:

"I love you, and I want to do it."
"You don't love me. If you loved me, you wouldn't be pressuring me to do something I'm not ready for."

"C'mon, everybody gets drunk at least once."
"I'm not everybody. Maybe I'm just stronger."

Adolescents practice these lines in classrooms and gain skills in turning around the pressure. But I worry that these skills, which students may demonstrate with perfection in school, are not used nearly as well in real life. The problem is that teenagers' desire to fit in is likely to be in direct conflict with their desire *not* to engage in a particular activity. They may want to refuse or reject something but not burn their bridges by cutting off a friend or peer in any way that appears too final or confrontational.

For example, when a boy tells a girl that he loves her, the last thing that she wants to say is in effect "No, you don't." When a teenager is told "Everybody is doing it," the last thing he may want to say is "I'm not everybody." I think, therefore, that we should continue to teach *both* the firm reverse-the-pressure strategy when it is necessary to reject flatly any dangerous proposition and other ways to go when the situation is less harmful or the child wants to maintain some relationship.

We can strive for this effective, realistic goal: teach young teens how to state a position clearly ("No, I won't") without ending the friendship entirely. In other words, "the subject is nonnegotiable, but we can continue to be friends." To reach this goal, we can show them two follow-up steps to a firm refusal that do not burn all their bridges. After responding to the first line immediately and clearly, teenagers have these options:

- Reasonable conversation about what they want (something else to do)

- Reversal of pressure if they are in a situation where they are comfortable putting the other teen in his or her place

An example of the reasonable-conversation option would go like this:

"I love you, too, and I'm glad you love me. Still, having sex isn't going to make that love stronger if only one of us is ready."

And an example of the reverse-the-pressure option would be a response like:

"You know, if you really loved me, you wouldn't pressure me about this."

These follow-up options are not used to back down from the clear, strong refusal to accept the line. They should not erase the period at the end of the sentence or replace it with a question mark. And they do not reopen the door to negotiation, but they can soften the blow or extend the discussion of why the teenager will not buy into the line.

Let's consider how another line will run its course:

LINE: "You're so hot. I can't stop myself. I really want to do it."

TYPICAL RESPONSE: "Oh, I feel hot when I'm with you. You're hot, too. I just don't want to go any further right now."

Guess what? That teenager will cave. That teenager will have sex.

A better response would be, "Thank you, but we're still not doing it." (Can you hear the period at the end of that sentence?)

Then, follow-up responses such as, "You turn me on. I think I feel as strongly about you, but still I know I'm not ready for this. Let's figure out what we can do that we're both comfortable with" (the conversational reply). Or, "I feel much less hot when I feel pressured" (the reverse-the-pressure reply).

The same skills of recognizing a line and its underlying motive and responding firmly with no room for negotiation can be practiced for drug use scenarios:

LINE: "Oh, come on. Everybody does this stuff. Just once. How will you know if you like it or not unless you try it?"

TYPICAL RESPONSE: "Well, I don't know. I don't think I should . . . " (Yes, this kid will experiment.)

THE STRONGER, IMMEDIATE REPLY: "I don't want to do drugs, dude." The conversational follow-up possibility: "Look, I know you're my friend. I want to hang out with you—just not when you're high. When you're straight, let's play basketball. I'll probably still be at the courts."

AND THE REVERSE-THE-PRESSURE POSSIBILITY: "Do you do everything people tell you to do? Are you everybody? I gotta tell you, you're a good guy, but I hope you change before you get really messed up."

Big Hint

The dialogues I have sketched are intended only to give you ideas and suggestions. Please do not rattle them off verbatim or your kids will say you sound corny or "It's not like that." But once you have gone over these dialogues and absorbed their general tone and structure, try to communicate the ideas in as few words as possible. Guide your kids to fill in the various parts (line, typical response, firm response, and follow-ups) with their own language. You set up the scenario, but then stick to brief, general phrases. Ask them to respond with clear messages that end in a period and allow for no negotiation.

When they do a good job in supplying those firm responses, praise them, but do not stop there. Go on to ask how they can follow up: "All right, how could you turn that pressure right back on the person?" or "Great reply. Now suppose you want to keep your relationship going, but you also want control of the situation. How would you handle that?"

As a practice exercise, consider how you will prepare your child to deal successfully with lines like these:

"Everyone else is doing it."

"Want a hit? It will make you feel good."

"It's not as good with condoms . . . I'm OK; I'm clean; don't worry . . . Don't you trust me?"

"If you loved me, you would do it."

"C'mon, one drink won't hurt you."

"It's OK with me if you don't do it; that's more for me. Loser."

"If you cut school with us today, no one will even notice. They'll just think you're sick. Besides, I think you are ready to begin hanging out with us now."

Shift the Blame

Wouldn't it be wonderful if our children would avoid all risky behaviors because they have a clear sense of right and wrong?

They would feel so strongly about safe, responsible behaviors that whenever they are confronted with negative pressures they would emphatically say, "No, I will not do this. I am morally, spiritually, and ethically opposed to that behavior!"

In our dreams. Unfortunately, this will not happen. Young people do not climb up on a moral soapbox and confront their friends for one simple reason. They are so tightly connected to their friends and they so desperately seek peers' approval that they dare not oppose them.

Ironic, isn't it, when you think of how confrontational they can be toward *you*? They will not only oppose and argue with you, but they are pretty good at it! "You're ruining my life . . . You're always trying to run my life . . . Everything would be perfect if you'd just leave me alone . . . You treat me like a baby and don't trust me . . ."

Kids this age talk that way to you and about you among their friends. Mom and Dad are the enemies, the fun-spoilers, the nags, the cops, the snoops. That is how young teens typically describe their parents to their friends.

This can be quite upsetting to a loving parent. It hurts, but remember that this is developmentally normal. They need to break away from you over the next several years, and this is a typical way for them to start that process.

So you are the enemy who is always throwing a wet blanket on all their fun. Great! Use this! Let your children shift the blame to you. This is a face-saving way for them to avoid danger or get out of a trouble spot.

But you first have to tell them that this is OK and show them how to do it. Pick a time when things are calm (not during or right after a confrontation). Tell them up front that you are willing to be the bad guy, the heavy—and their friends will never need to know. Then teach them two highly effective techniques: using a code word and creating a rumor.

Develop a Code Word

Your child and you agree on a code word or phrase that will only be used in an emergency. Let your child select the word or phrase. The two ground rules are straightforward:

1. The code should not be shared with anyone else—including your child's best friend.

2. The code should *only* be used in a potentially dangerous situation or an emergency. It's an SOS—a real cry to be rescued from a harmful spot.

Make certain that you and your child understand what *emergency* and *potentially dangerous situation* mean. We are not just talking about extremes. It does not have to be an abduction by a pervert. We are not talking only about kidnapping or life-threatening circumstances. Instead, it should be understood that *emergency* and *dangerous situations* can refer to any occasion when your child feels uncomfortable or at risk and cannot get to safety on his or her own.

Do some brainstorming about what these situations could be. Suggestion: Your child is at a friend's house and other kids show up. A spontaneous party begins. No adult is at home. A keg of beer appears. Some older kids bring bongs. Your child wants to get out of there fast but doesn't want the others to see her as a wimp.

When you and your children understand the various situations that call for a code word, you can teach them how to apply it. Here are the guidelines and the script:

1. Your child never goes anywhere without enough coins for a phone call.

2. When in a challenging spot, your young teen finds a way to call you, complaining all the time to friends about how unreasonable it is that she has to check in with her horribly demanding parents.

3. She phones you in the presence of her friends and casually slips in the code word to inform you that she is in trouble and needs to shift the blame to you. She might say something like, "What's up? (code phrase) Yeah, I'm at Steve's. I know I'm late. I'll be home soon."

4. You act angry and speak loudly enough for her friends to hear you through the phone. "What do you mean by checking in now! You were supposed to call home at eight, Kelsey! Did you forget you were supposed to be here to see your cousins? They've been waiting two hours for you! GET HOME RIGHT THIS MINUTE!"

5. If Kelsey can get a ride home safely, she will hang up and complain to her friends that you—her mean, screeching, nasty parent—have ruined her life yet again.

6. If Kelsey cannot get home safely—say, her friends do not drive or those with a license have been drinking—she can cre-

ate a situation for you to come and drag her away. She would yell into the phone, "What do you mean, I have to come home right this minute? I don't have to listen to you."

That is her signal to let you know this is her final plea, and she needs you to come and get her. So you demand, "What is Steve's address? I'm coming to get you now. You'd better be out in front of Steve's house or else!" After she hangs up, she can again complain to her friends about how mean and nasty her parents are. She has gotten herself out of a jam successfully by shifting the blame to you and still maintaining her position as one of the crowd.

7. When she is safely home, you should praise her for using the code word technique and carrying out the prearranged plan so well.

Never punish a child for getting into a dangerous situation because that could discourage or prevent her from ever coming back to you for help in another crisis. Tell her how proud you are of her for being so cool and responsible in a tough spot, but also discuss strategies for avoiding similar situations in the future. Then you both may want to change the code word so she can use it again.

Students Against Driving Drunk (SADD) has a contract that is designed to support teens in difficult situations, particularly being stuck without a sober ride home. This contract, which teenagers and parents sign, has had a real impact. (See Resources, page 215, for SADD listing.) If a teenager has private access to a phone, it can work perfectly. But it is difficult for a teen who is drinking with his friends to say, "Gee, fellas, we've all screwed up. I'm going to call my Mom now for a ride

home." For this reason, I will not sign a driver's license physical exam unless I have given a teenager the SADD contract *and*
taught him how to use a code word for his parent's help.

Create a Rumor

When a group of friends expect certain behaviors of each other,
it is particularly difficult for individual kids to change that
behavior even when they want to change or disregard it.

For example, consider Eddie: Early in fifth grade, Eddie's
friends began to act out in school—talking back to teachers,
coaches, and parents. Eddie tried to keep up with their language and attitudes. He felt uncomfortable about it, but desperately wishing to be accepted by the others, he learned a
litany of disrespectful words. By the end of fifth grade, Eddie
had quite a reputation. Despite numerous reprimands and punishments by parents and teachers, Eddie was in so deep that
he did not know *how* to change without losing status among
his peers.

Or take Omar as another example. He is the class clown.
He has been eagerly awaiting puberty while his friends have
soared ahead in size and development. Omar cannot compete
on the football field. Girls are not noticing him. Suddenly,
becoming the class clown gets him a lot of attention. It is a difficult cycle to break.

Much the same thing happens when teens want to quit
smoking, using drugs, shoplifting, or cutting classes. They
began smoking cigarettes or marijuana to win approval and
acceptance from friends. Or they acquired a cool reputation by
starting to cut classes in eighth grade. As these behaviors continue, young teens may want to stop the pattern, but they fear

that giving up this expected behavior will cost them those friendships.

There is a way out, by shifting the blame to the parent. For instance, kids seeking peer approval by acting out in school will acquire a Bad Girl or Bad Boy reputation. They may secretly want to drop the act but don't know how. They can create a rumor that the principal has been calling their parents and threatening suspension. They can tell their friends that their parents have laid down the law. Now they have an acceptable reason to tone down the offending behavior.

A child can create a rumor or tell a white lie by complaining to friends that he or she has been *forced* to give up certain behaviors by parents who have lowered the boom. "I'll be grounded for a month if they catch me cursing or if the teacher calls and tells them what I said in school," Eddie could say. Or Omar might say, as he clowns around after school but not during class, "Are you kidding? If my father gets one more call complaining that I'm messing up the class, I'm gonna get sent to some dweeb school! Have you ever tried living with my parents?"

Another example: A young teen can create a rumor that his parents have caught him smoking marijuana. He can tell his peers, "Now they check me every time I come home. My mom looks in my eyes, sniffs my clothes. She's all over me. And my dad has been threatening me with drug tests. They say if they catch me again, they won't let me get my license when I turn sixteen."

I have worked with several adolescents who have blamed me. I have told asthmatic teens to tell their friends that their doctor said they could end up in the hospital if they smoked. One young man, who had chest pain when he did cocaine, worried that drugs had injured him permanently. I reassured him that his heart was OK, but he decided to tell his friends that his doctor said he had weakened his heart and it couldn't take any more cocaine. His friends backed him up and protected him from those who were still passing around drugs.

These strategies work effectively because friends are sympathetic. They can relate to mean, punitive, overly controlling parents. Adolescents do not have to worry about losing status or peers' approval because adults are clearly the bad guys. They may even find that their friends will back them up.

Practice Means Prevention

Now it is time to practice these techniques with your child. Review the entire strategy of selecting and using a code word. Demonstrate how parents can be used to create a rumor to get a child out of a difficult situation. Ask your son or daughter to practice various rumors in front of you so that they sound believable. Here are some examples to get you both started:

> "I can't go with you tonight because my parents said I will be grounded this weekend unless I finish my history homework."

> "I can't buy cigarettes. The woman behind the counter knows my mom from church."

> "My father drives by that park on his way home from work. With my luck, he'll be sure to see us."

> "I have to get home 'cause my parents are dragging me to a family outing early tomorrow morning."

"No, thanks. Alcohol (or smoking) messes up my asthma medication, and my parents will know something is going on if I start wheezing."

"I can't cut school with you. My dad drops me off and then circles round the building to be sure I've gone inside."

"I gotta get home to watch my bratty little brother 'cause my mom calls and checks to see if I'm there."

"I can't drink or smoke with you guys because my mother will smell it on me."

Here is a common situation that shows the significance of a peer influence and how to help a child deal with it:

Parents often bring a preteen to see me when he or she starts failing in school. Mr. and Mrs. S. were alarmed because their son James was failing eighth grade. They wondered whether he might have a learning disability. My first question in this situation is always, "Is this school failure new and sudden or has it been going on for some time?" In their son's case, it was new. James had been a solid B student, with an occasional C, who suddenly was flunking all his subjects. When school failure is new, I consider these possibilities: a negative peer group, drug use, anxiety, depression, or discord at home that makes the child unable to concentrate on schoolwork.

When I asked James what was going on, his initial response was a very common one: "I'm just lazy. I'll fix it. I'll bring up my grades next marking period." But as we talked privately, he confided that he had changed schools and fallen in with a peer group that used drugs and considered good grades very uncool.

He wanted to be accepted, so he started experimenting with drugs. When I talked with him, he had stopped using drugs, but his peers were rejecting him—"You think you're better than we are" was their retort. James became ambivalent and somewhat depressed. He started cutting classes to prove to his friends that he didn't consider himself better than they were.

How to turn this situation around? James and I talked over several possibilities, similar to the refusal skills discussed earlier in this chapter, and we came up with a strategy: he could blame his parents as the Bad Guys by telling his friends, "I gotta go to class because my parents are on my case ever since the teachers have been calling them . . . If I flunk algebra and history again, my parents are going to send me to a different school . . . I can't do drugs with you 'cause my mom and dad check me every time I come home . . ."

A key part of this strategy involved his parents. I discussed with the family the importance of supporting a more positive peer group. James had begun to pull away from the negative kids and, over the summer, spent more time with some neighborhood friends who were positive influences. I explained to Mr. and Mrs. S. how critical it was for them to provide opportunities for these positive friendships to flourish in order for James to get back on track. They readily understood and came up with ideas that allowed James to spend more time with these new friends.

The third part of this overall strategy involved a way for James to re-earn his parents' trust. We discussed a contract by which Mr. and Mrs. S. would check his grades and confer with his teachers to be sure his schoolwork was improving. In turn, James would earn greater privileges as he won back their trust. (You'll find more about such contracts in Chapter 9.)

Let's conclude this chapter with a typical but worrisome example of the influence of peers:

Drugs are available in every small town, suburb, and city today. I see many young patients who want to stop doing drugs but, largely because of peer pressure, find themselves unable to do so because their "friends" set them up to fail. These friends lead them to believe that they want to include them in all the fun. Because allegiance to peers is paramount at this age, many young people will sacrifice their personal progress to join their friends. To be a real friend, they conclude, they should go along with the fun. They do not understand their peers' underlying motivation: to drag them down.

With young people who want to change their behavior, I have the following choreographed conversation to help them prepare themselves for this challenge:

ME: Let me ask you, Mike, how do your friends feel about getting high?

MIKE: Good.

ME: I don't mean *while* they're doing drugs. How do they feel about using drugs when they're not high?

MIKE: I guess they feel bad.

ME: But if they think everybody's doing it, do they really have a reason to feel bad?

MIKE: No, 'cause it's normal. It's just what kids do.

ME: But what if they realize that not all kids do it? It's not normal. They have a choice. How would they feel then?

MIKE: Bad. Maybe guilty.

ME: Right. So when you quit drugs, how does it make your friends feel?

MIKE: Guilty, because they'd realize you don't *have* to do it.

ME: And why do you think they try so hard to get you to do drugs with them?

MIKE: So they don't have to feel bad about themselves.

ME: Yes. Well, Mike, how can you be a really good friend?

MIKE: Wow! I could be a role model for my friends if I didn't do it. (The cognitive Ah-Ha! kicks in.)

ME: Exactly!

6

Helping Your Child Cope with Stress

Let's talk about stress briefly. This is one of the shortest chapters in the book but potentially the most important because it can have the longest-lasting effect on your children if you take it to heart. Many adults think that stress is strictly an adult problem. Believe me, it's not. Kids today are *very stressed out*. Like adults, they feel the physical and emotional consequences of chronic stress.

It's fairly simple; contemporary life is stressful. Stress makes us uncomfortable, tense, tired, worn out. We feel as though we need or want to run away, to escape the immediate pressure, or at least to forget about it. It is no different for young people. The critical question is: how do they deal with it?

All parents' greatest desire is to steer their children away from harmful behaviors and toward a safer, productive future.

By making them aware of the consequences of certain behaviors, you are taking an important step toward protecting your children. By showing them the skills to avoid or reject those behaviors, you have done even more. But despite parents' best efforts, many kids will occasionally try some risky behaviors that we wish they would avoid. When they do experiment with worrisome behaviors, they can take one of two directions: they may try it and then move on with the rest of their lives with a "been there, done that" attitude, or they may get stuck in a risky lifestyle.

When kids feel under stress, they want those uncomfortable feelings to go away. Will they cope with a quick, easy fix or with a positive, real solution? Their ability to deal with stress is the key factor in determining which way they will go. Parents can most effectively protect children from falling into a risky lifestyle by making sure that a child does not *need* to get stuck in a cycle of negative behaviors. Young people will not get caught in that cycle if they see a positive future for themselves and are able to cope with life's adversities.

Let's face it, any negative behavior fills a need, right? Just walk through a cloud of smoke outside any office building in midafternoon—stressed-out employees are filling their need to get away from their desks and relieve daily workplace tension.

When people fall into patterns of negative behaviors to relieve stress, how can they break the pattern? If you try to get someone to change a negative behavior without understanding the context in which the behavior is needed—the void it fills— you will fail. If other alternatives to filling that need are missing, there is little hope for change.

Many of the negative behaviors so feared by parents often mask real, underlying problems. For example, drugs mask all sorts of emotional issues like stress, anxiety, or difficulty concentrating; eating disorders provide a sense of control; fighting relieves anger, gives a feeling of power, and may cover up a real sense of helplessness; sex, if only for a moment, makes someone feel loved; affiliating with a gang makes a young person feel protected, connected, and even loved; dropping out of school may relieve a student of school-related anxiety. All of these troubling behaviors actually work very effectively in coping with stress—at least in the short term.

Look at the illustration on page 122. Everyone experiences stress. Everyone needs to cope with it in some way. The negative strategies are often the quick, easy fixes, but they are *negative* because they all have long-term consequences that harm the individual or society.

A parent's most important job may be to assure that his or her child has a wide repertoire of positive coping strategies from which to choose when confronted with stress. When parents provide a wide array of positive alternatives, they give their children a priceless gift that will last a lifetime.

In the following paragraphs, I will suggest various components in this wide repertoire you can provide your children. But the foundation is your own approach for coping with stress in your life. As we have discussed, modeling is vital. Your preteens are watching you. If you smoke to relax, drink after a hard day's work, or vent road rage, do not be surprised when your child starts to smoke, take drugs, or hit a little brother. On the other hand, if you model positive coping strategies, your children will see the positive results. If they hear you talking with friends to find solutions to personal problems, see you exercising on a regular basis, and making time for yourself, you can expect your children to buffer themselves against adversity.

Stress and Coping Strategies

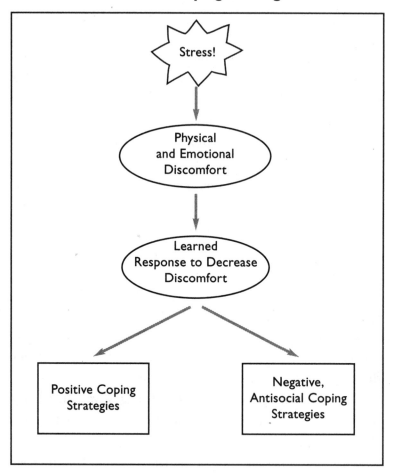

When you model positive coping strategies, you are helping yourself and your children. As we consider several strategies please keep in mind that the wide variety of constructive
alternatives you will be showing your children has to be tai-
lored personally. The strategies you choose will depend on your
value system, your community, and your child's likes and dis-
likes. I hope you will spend some time thinking about these
vital components.

Universal Coping Strategies

One of the most apparent strategies—and one that is often overlooked because it is so obvious—is *talking*. Parents have immense control over how a preteen perceives this most basic positive coping mechanism. If you make yourself available as a real listener, you can teach your child the value of talking things out with other people. Your child will learn that uncorking bottled-up worries can make a big difference in lowering her stress level. Even more beneficial, if she can develop some solutions to her problems when guided by a trusted, willing listener, she will learn to think and talk things through carefully before she reacts impulsively.

Another universal positive coping strategy is *exercise*. It really does reduce stress. I explain this to young teens with this simple biology lesson:

If a tiger was coming at you, you would be pretty stressed out, right? It would make your heart beat fast. Every fiber of your body would say *run!!!* It wouldn't be a good time to concentrate on your homework, would it? Well, not very many tigers will be chasing you, but there are a lot of other things that can stress you out. They make our bodies feel like a tiger is about to chase us. In fact, a hormone called adrenaline goes all through our bodies and tells us when there is a real emergency. It warns us that we'd better get ready to deal with it or else! So what do you think is a good way of dealing with it? I'll give you a hint—your body is saying *run!* That's right—*run!*

I teach kids that the times when they are the most stressed are the times when they should run (or exercise) the hardest. And I encourage them to exercise on a regular basis to get rid of all the leftover hormones. (The same can be said to adults: "You think you don't have time to exercise? Well, I'll tell you that you don't have time *not* to exercise.")

The tiger analogy is helpful as a lead-in to another universal positive coping strategy: *deep breathing and visualization.* Biology lesson Number Two explains it:

So, remember the tiger coming at you? Your body is screaming, *run!* Your body prepares to take off. All of a sudden, your breathing gets heavier and faster. Your heart beats faster. Your blood rushes to your legs so you can be ready to run. You know that feeling of butterflies in your stomach when you get nervous? That sensation is actually the blood leaving your gut so that your leg muscles prepare to sprint. Now, if a tiger really is racing toward you, you should run! But if it just *feels* that way, here are two ways to make you feel better:

We've talked about the first—you have to exercise. The second is to fool your body into thinking that you're relaxed. You can turn off the adrenaline so you can think clearly and calmly. The easiest way to do this is to do the *opposite* of what you would do if you literally were getting ready to run.

- Instead of standing or sitting up straight, recline in a position that says "no emergency here."

- Stop focusing on the problem. Close your eyes instead, and think of something very relaxing—perhaps your favorite spot or any place where you can chill out, as long as it's not a WWF match!

- Finally, slow down your breathing. Take deep, slow breaths in. Hold them. Feel the burn and then let them out slooooooowly. Do this several times.

(By the way, I use this breathing technique to help teens quit smoking. I explain that half of the relaxation comes from the drag, and if they like that, they can have the drag without the poison and absolutely free.)

Learning how to control the body's stress reactions can be used to avoid the loss of control that occurs with stress. As shown by the following story, a young person can use this positive coping strategy to reverse a behavioral problem.

Randy was developing a reputation for backtalk and rudeness in school. His parents brought him to see me because teachers and the principal had been calling them with increasing frequency. As Randy and I talked, I discovered that he was trapped in a cycle: his behavior was leading teachers to *expect* him to behave badly, though he secretly didn't enjoy this Bad Boy tag. One particular teacher was trying to out-tough Randy by challenging him and upping the ante. Whenever Randy blurted out a sarcastic remark in class, the teacher got in his face and loudly threatened to send him to the principal's office the next time Randy opened his mouth. Not wanting to back down in front of his classmates, Randy predictably fell into the trap and uttered another smart one-liner, and so the cycle perpetuated itself.

I asked Randy, "Who's winning? When the teacher puts you in that position and you respond that way, the teacher wins by proving you're a Bad Kid, right?" We talked about ways for Randy to win—to be more an adult than the teacher. I described how the body acts when it is about to fight. ("You stand up, your muscles tighten, you breathe faster, and you raise your voice.") Then I explained how actively choosing to do the opposite would give Randy control and help him stay calm when the teacher got on his case.

"Instead of standing up, face to face, when the teacher comes close to you, sit down in a relaxed position. Take deep, slow breaths so your stress hormones don't kick in," I said.

Randy learned that he could remain calm, think without reacting from his gut, and even reply to the teacher in an even, qui-
eter voice without rudeness. Although his friends taunted him
for a day or two, Randy's reputation among his classmates actually went up several notches because they saw him as cool and
strong. They watched him respond in a mature way and recognized that he was the winner of this conflict.

Doctor's Orders

The next coping strategy is probably the most difficult for
adults to accept: It is OK to take care of yourself. This coping
technique is vital for you to model for your own well-being and
for the good of your adolescent. No matter how busy life
becomes, parents need to have some "me time" every day—
time when you do not have to think about problems, time to
stop worrying about friends, work, or family. It only needs to
be a short time, but it should be pleasurable and selfish. During "me time," you may want to read, watch a game, soak in a
candlelit bath, or sip a cup of tea. Whatever you choose to do,
keep this time protected. Use it to unwind and "unworry."

Make this special time a daily habit, and think of it as a
gift you give yourself and your children. By modeling a relaxation strategy, you show them that everyone deserves some time
to be purely selfish. You send the message that unwinding in
this way can rejuvenate us so we can gather energy to deal with
life's tribulations. (This can be particularly important to model
for daughters because girls too often get the message that
women are supposed to take care of everyone else ahead of
themselves.)

If you are thinking, "Oh, right, there's no way I can take this selfish time for myself," stop for a moment and look at it this way: it is really not selfish; consider it a *selfless* act to demonstrate positive coping skills to your children. That's a doctor's order from me: take and enjoy some of your own space and pleasure!

Other Ways of Coping

In addition to the universal positive coping strategies already suggested, a variety of others are available for individuals to tailor to their own needs and preferences. They may include:

Prayer	Music
Poetry	Studying
Hobbies	Dancing
Art	Volunteering

Volunteering may take some explanation. One of the best ways to cope with problems is by helping others with theirs. Even more, one of the most effective ways to make your son or daughter believe that they have value is by helping them realize that they can make a difference as an individual. Many young adolescents, who quite naturally become caught up in their own worries about school, popularity, clothes, and other self-centered concerns, get a boost of self-esteem when they tutor younger children, or sing with a youth choir at a nursing home, or participate in an environmental cleanup of the neighborhood park.

Getting Kids Unstuck

Don't wait until your children are teenagers to demonstrate a wide variety of coping strategies. Start today, no matter how young they are.

When kids do get in trouble and use negative coping techniques, there are ways to help them get unstuck. The method is based on the same positive, preventive ideas that we have discussed above. Here is an example: When I met Jay, he was seventeen and highly intelligent. His father was also bright, but he had a history of drug addiction. Jay came across with a very laid-back facade, so laid-back, in fact, that he determined that he no longer needed to attend school. And so laid-back that he did his share of drugs—to relax, he said.

I began our conversation this way: "Some kids I know use drugs because they think being high is fun. But most kids I know take drugs because it takes away some sort of bad feeling, like stress, sadness, or nervousness."

Then I asked Jay the most important question for anyone on drugs: "How about you? Why do you take drugs?"

"Because they make me chill."

I learned that Jay was taking a prescription anxiety medication that he was getting from a dealer. This was a major clue that he was likely to be self-treating an anxiety disorder. As I asked him more questions, it became clear that he was dropping out of school because he was so anxious about it. I did not condemn him for his drug use. Instead, I looked at it in the context of his life. I even praised him for being smart enough to have picked a drug that a doctor might prescribe. But after a pause and a deep breath, I told Jay that no doctor would give him the medication for more than two days straight because of how addictive it can be.

"Don't worry. I have it under control," he said. "I pop only two, maybe three, pills a week."

"This is the most important day of your life, Jay," I said, "because it is the day you will decide if you are going to be a drug addict."

"No problem. I'm not. Decision made. I can handle it."

I asked Jay how he thought his father got addicted.

Jay responded strongly. "He just couldn't handle it."

Then I drew the stress diagram for Jay. I explained how taking drugs worked as a coping strategy in the short term and that's why people do drugs. "But let's suppose that someone uses drugs two, maybe three, times a week. They are 'under control.' No addiction there, just a great way to feel a little bit better, right?" I asked. "Well, what happens when that person has the worst week of his life? Maybe his girl broke up with him. Maybe his boss is on his case. He wants to cope with all this stress. And what has he learned works?"

"Drugs," Jay answered softly.

"Right. And on the worst week of his life, how much does he do then?"

"Lots."

"Right." Next I drew cycle after cycle on the diagram to illustrate how many times in a week that person would take drugs to cope during that worst week. Then I asked Jay how he thought people would respond to this person's being high all week long. Would his girlfriend and coworkers congratulate him for his wonderful coping strategy?

"Naw, they would be on his case even more."

"So, does this guy's stress then go up or down?"

"Up. Way up!" Jay answered.

"And how will he deal with that extra stress?"

"More drugs."

"Exactly. You see how no one plans to be a drug addict? They just get trapped. I never want this to happen to you. That's why I want you to know how to move in the other direction. Let's work on filling in this box with positive ways you can deal with your nervousness, OK?"

My point is simply this: experimentation may be a normal part of adolescence. We work hard to prevent children from even experimenting. But it is absolutely up to us to make certain that they do not become stuck in a negative, feel-good-for-the-moment behavioral pattern. If we truly want to prevent risk behaviors, we must help every child grow into the kind of person who doesn't need those negative behaviors to cope.

7

Other People as Reinforcements

Up to this point, you have learned the importance of offering a variety of strategies to give your child the best chance of choosing positive behaviors. As diligently as parents strive to teach and reinforce constructive choices and to deter children from moving toward negative ones, this fact remains: you and your child do not live in a hermetically sealed cocoon. When your child is out there in a real-world environment, all the good skills you have taught and practiced together will need continual reinforcement. And you will not—cannot—always be at your child's side. Yet for that reinforcement to be effective, it is necessary on an ongoing basis.

Add to that fact another basic one: during those few years between early childhood and mid- to late adolescence, a parent is usually the last person children want reinforcement from, or at least, that is what they will tell you. You are of utmost importance in their lives, though, so you should never feel powerless. It may seem contradictory, but early to mid-adolescents need more space from parents precisely because they feel so close to you—really! For the sake of your own sanity and self-esteem, learn to accept some of this developmentally normal rebellion. Remember that the fundamental job of an adolescent is to become independent from parents. Until recently, you have burped, diapered, and fed your children. They have relied heavily on you for homework help, transportation, and their sense of self-worth (which they still do, and will continue to do, by the way). But they have to pull away from you to achieve independence. Like lovers who break up, they need to go through a period of resenting you until they can stand on their own feet. So expect and allow this; you really have no other choice.

What else can you do? You certainly don't bow out of their lives completely. In fact, you can be as influential as ever but in more subtle ways. Visualize yourself as the casting director of a play or movie. You select particular people to play critical roles in your child's life. You can construct an environment of strong, positive influences—a team of friends, peers, older teenagers who are good role models, and other adults—to support and reinforce the good job that you are already doing. And here's where the subtlety comes in: your child doesn't need to know that you have deliberately enlisted these allies. Let's look first at your child's circle of friends and how you can influence it.

Friends and Activities

If you want to know more about preteens, learn about their friends. As unique as each child is, remember that this is the age of conflict and confusion. Each child strives to be independent, but they all want a sense of belonging, of connection, to their peer group. Just stroll through a mall and observe how they dress alike, talk alike, listen to similar music. Of course, there are different peer groups, so not all twelve-year-old girls wear neon nail polish. Not all boys shave their heads or pierce body parts. But whatever group a single child wants to join, you can be sure that this is the age of The Uniform. Kids adopt a look, a style, language, and an attitude to reflect their connection to some peer group.

Whether your child confides in you or says next to nothing about school and friends, you can gain insight into your child by getting to know his or her friends. The trick, though, is not to try. Do not try to be a pal or a contemporary. And do not query your child about friends. Both of those attempts are sure-fire failures. A good indicator that your child is passing through the gates of adolescence is the first time she says, "Leave my friends alone. They don't talk about *you* all the time," when you have just make an inconsequential (you thought) comment about one of her friends, such as "That was a pretty sweater Tasha was wearing."

Another typical comment from a preteen was uttered by Alex to his father after the last of Alex's friends had piled out of the car: "Pleeeeeease, Dad. Don't talk to my friends!" His father had only said, "Hi, how are you?" to the boys he was driving home. But Alex's reaction was common for a preteen: he thought his father's words were an inquisition. From Alex's thirteen-year-old perspective, his father was supposed to be the silent, invisible chauffeur.

When you are cast in a nonspeaking role like Alex's father, you can learn a great deal by listening and observing your child's friends. As you drive them around, you will pick up comments

and hints about their behavior. Do not comment at that time—
or your child will crawl under the seat from embarrassment. Just
keep your eyes and ears open. Pretend you are totally absorbed
in driving and watching the traffic. But store your observations.
Some of the information you gather will give you important
clues about behaviors your adolescent is, or may be in danger
of becoming, involved with.

Some observations will give you jumping-off points to
begin a conversation later with your child. For example, Jose's
father overheard one of his friends mention a neighborhood
store where clerks did not check IDs when underage kids
bought cigarettes. Instead of lecturing or threatening, Jose's
father casually brought up the subject the next evening in a choreographed conversation:

DAD: "I saw one of those signs 'We check IDs' at the con-
venience store this morning when I stopped to buy the
newspaper. Are those signs something new?"

JOSE: "I don't know . . . I guess so."

DAD: "Do you think they really keep kids under eighteen from buying cigarettes?"

JOSE: "Maybe . . ."

DAD: "I wonder what happens to store owners who sell
to underage kids."

JOSE: "They get in trouble. I heard they have to pay a big
fine."

DAD: "And what happens to the kids?"

JOSE: "They get reported. I know a kid who got caught."

DAD: "Oh, yeah? What happened to him?"

JOSE: "They called his parents and he got grounded for a week. But he found another store that will not rat on him."

DAD: "So now what do you think will happen?"

JOSE: "Well, that store might get busted and he could get caught again. Then he'd be in really big trouble, I guess."

DAD: "So do you think he's taking a big chance?"

JOSE: "Yeah. I wouldn't try it."

By broaching the subject indirectly, Jose's father structured his agenda in such a way that Jose thought about the situation and came to his own conclusion, a far more effective lesson than if Dad had jumped into the conversation when Jose's friends were talking. If he had broken in to say, "That's really awful. Kids shouldn't be able to buy cigarettes anywhere. The clerk ought to be arrested!" Jose would have been embarrassed in front of his peers, probably would have become resentful or angry at his father, and would have missed the opportunity to think about the situation and draw a smart, safe conclusion.

Listen to Their Stories

Preteens are more inclined to talk about their friends than older adolescents, though they still will keep certain information from you. And that's OK. It is important for them to feel they own private information. When friends confide in them, they learn to trust and be trusted. You want to encourage your children to honor those expressions of trust, but you also need to let them know that if a friend is in real or potential trouble, they can be a better friend by talking to an adult than by keeping a dangerous secret. Again, you can get this lesson across most effectively by using the role-playing or choreographed conversation techniques that were explained in Chapter 4.

In less critical situations, when preteens are not entrusted with a friend's privacy, they often open up with stories—funny stories, silly stories, even boring stories, punctuated with plenty of adolescent phrases including "like" and "you know." You can learn a lot if you remember these guidelines:

- Pay attention when your child tells stories about friends.

- Really listen for the facts as well as the nuances.

- Let your preteen complete the story before you say anything.

- Express interest (even if you're not particularly entranced by every gossipy tidbit).

- Withhold judgment. Rather than saying something like "He's trouble. He's no good. Stay away from him," make a neutral statement that gets your child thinking, such as "Wow, I am really worried that he could get in over his head. How do you think he should handle that?" or "How would you handle a similar situation?" Statements like these can lead right into role-playing and choreographed conversations.

Beyond Listening

In addition to observing and listening, several other strategies can also help you understand your children's peer group and influence their choice of friends:

Make your home a welcome place for your child's friends. You do not have to buy the biggest screen TV or turn your house into a video arcade, but you can make kids feel comfortable. A few popular snack foods will help, but a more important ingredient is your attitude. It is most effective if you are friendly without hovering or asking too many questions. You want your child's friends to know that you are in the house and available but you will also stay in the background for the most part. You can offer to feed them supper or drive them home or to a movie, but it is helpful to check with your child first in case he or she doesn't want you to make these offers.

A word of caution: Some parents try so hard to be pals with their kids' friends that they overdo it. They act too cool, which adolescents instantly detect as phony. Or they attempt to be so hospitable—perhaps to enhance their child's popularity—that they let down all limits. Parents who fall into this pattern are often the ones whose liquor cabinets are raided when they are asleep upstairs. Or they are so *laissez-faire* that older teenagers crash their homes and stage parties when parents are out of the house. These are the parents who return home to find that neighbors have called the police or the police have actually taken teenagers into custody, or worse.

Choose your child's friends. Do you think you read that incorrectly? Choose your child's friends? *No way she'd let me,* you're thinking.

That is true. Preteens and teenagers certainly do not want or allow parents to select their friends any more than they want you to choose their clothes or hairstyles. If you try to pick their friends for them, chances are that they will instantly dislike your choices. Or they will befriend kids whom you disapprove of or forbid them to see.

Long gone are the nursery school days when you could arrange "play dates" with certain children whom you liked or whose parents were friends of yours. It is impossible to choose friends actively, so do not go at it from that direction, but you can *influence* your child's choice of friends. You can make it easier for them to hang out with a group whose values and behaviors mesh with yours and to avoid others who may be negative influences. Here are five suggestions:

1. Do not dictate friendships. Do not say, "I want you to hang around more often with Sankey. He's such a good kid." As soon as you say that, you have condemned Sankey to dorkdom in your child's view.

2. Do not forbid friendships. If you were to say, "Stop hanging out with Jeremy. He's nothing but trouble," Jeremy would immediately become intriguing and mysterious—forbidden fruit. If you know for a fact that a certain friend or classmate is really trouble, you can make this a strong suggestion, but you

will need to take some steps to back it up. First, make sure that your child has other positive friends in place. If you try to separate him from a worrisome peer but the only option is isolation, you will lose. In the rare situation when another child poses a true danger to yours, then you certainly have a responsibility to separate them. Make your fears clear to your child. Prepare him by showing him a way of separating while still saving face (as in "shifting the blame," Chapter 4). Finally, back it up with consequences that allow your child to shift the blame to you (see Chapter 9 for ways to put this situation into a safety/responsibility contract).

3. Foster the good friendships by making contact easier. Be more available to offer rides or host a sleepover when you want your child to spend time with kids who are positive influences. For example, you may want to let your daughter skip some chores to have dinner at Shari's home when you know that Shari and her family are good influences. Be more willing to drive your daughter and Shari to a game or school play, especially when Shari's parents cannot. In other words, find ways to support the positive friendships.

4. Encourage your child to join activities or youth groups where you know that good values are promoted and reinforced.

5. Use the power of the dollar. Open your wallet a bit to encourage positive relationships to develop and grow, but subtly explain that money is tight when it comes to events and equipment that are associated with a negative peer group. For example, Peter hangs out with two crowds, the basketball play-

ers and the football players. After basketball games, that group hangs out, talks, goes to the food court, and comes home to study because the coach insists on good grades. The football crowd hangs out on corners and is known to use drugs. So Peter's parents have a simple choice: they encourage him to play basketball. They buy him the right shoes. They keep the car out of the driveway so he and his friends can shoot hoops at the basket hanging above the garage door. They drive him to league games and save some extra money to enroll him in a summer basketball camp.

Get to know the parents of your child's friends. This is another extremely valuable way to influence your child's circle of friends and help them grow safe and strong together. Make informal alliances with other parents. Check in with them to be certain that an adult will be at home when your preteen plans to visit or stay overnight. When you work hand-in-hand with other parents, you will enjoy the additional support and camaraderie that is so important to both children and parents. Kids will be safer when there is a wider net of support, and you will not have the feeling of being the only parent in the world who is trying to protect your child.

Here's a real life example: Parents of several preteen girls decided to build strength in numbers before serious adolescent problems arose. The parents did not know each other well, though their daughters were all close friends.

One parent described how their alliance came about: "There was no specific crisis that brought us together, but a sense that our daughters were increasingly facing risky situations, especially alcohol at parties and all the stuff that goes with that. We knew that we needed to support each other and, if possible, present a somewhat united front to our daughters in terms of our beliefs and rules."

The parents of one girl, whom they felt was beginning to "get out of hand," invited six other parents to come over for coffee and a chat. At first, the parents who called the meeting took a harder line about telling other parents anything heard or seen about any child's behavior. But after some discussion, the first couple came around to what became the "majority" position that centered on three basic points:

1. Each parent agreed to help any child in need without repercussions. In other words, a girl can call on any friend's parent if she is in trouble without worrying about being punished or "turned in" to her own parents.

2. When any parent sees low- to midlevel risky behavior, he or she will first confront the child involved and warn her that if it happens again, "I will have to tell your parents."

3. If a behavior is life-threatening, a parent will go immediately to the girl's parents to inform them.

In reaching this agreement, the parents struggled with a major issue: how to continue holding their own child's trust while still looking out for the other girls. If one girl—call her Deirdre, for instance—told her mother something about her friend Selene, and Deirdre's mother went to Selene's parents, Deirdre probably would not tell her own mother much in the future. The group could not reach total agreement about the issue of trust, but one parent made a strong pitch for keeping confidentiality about news that their children told them unless it was health- or life-threatening. On the other hand, this parent maintained, the adults would not necessarily have to keep confidentiality if they themselves *saw* risky behaviors.

The trust/confidentiality issue was not resolved at the first meeting, but the parents who attended concluded that it was such an honest and fruitful gathering that they decided to continue getting together from time to time.

You are probably wondering what the girls thought about this parental rendezvousing to discuss their behaviors. Their first response was mutual horror, but by the time the meeting was actually held, the girls began suggesting other parents who should attend!

I relate this example simply to give you one idea about collaborating with parents of your child's friends. You may not agree with every part of the agreement that this group of parents reached. You may have other opinions and issues, but the point is to reach out and get to know parents of your child's friends. Communicate, share concerns, stay in touch, and support each other for the sake of all children involved.

Other Responsible Adults

Adults are very important in the lives of adolescents. While you, Mom or Dad, remain the most important of all adults, you are also the only one that your child is so focused on disagreeing with! (After all, your young adolescent doesn't have to break away from Great Aunt Sallie or Noah's father and mother.) So make sure that there are more "agreeable" adults around to be constructive influences and solid role models.

Think back to your own adolescence. Do you recall that your parents were the most popular of all the parents you knew? Did you think they were the most reasonable? (OK, I admit— I know your answer to that one.) Didn't you believe that some of your friends had really cool, reasonable parents? Maybe your Mom or Dad was more strict and demanding than your best friend's parents—the laid-back adults who were always willing to drive a carload of kids to and from school events, or take you for burgers after the basketball game? Do you recall how much more fun it was to ride around in their yellow convertible than your mother's dark sedan that resembled an unmarked police car? Do you remember feeling you could talk to a friend's parent more openly than to your own?

Teenagers need adults in their lives, more adults than just one or two parents. Young adolescents actually *respect* adults, though not always their own parents. They are curious about how other adults think and act. And they can be highly influenced by adults other than their parents.

You may begin to hear your preteens expressing different political views from those they have always heard at home. They may start to question your standards about spending and saving money, attending religious services, or taking vacations together as a family. Where is this coming from? you wonder. Not only from their peers, but from observing friends' parents and other adults in their lives.

Once again, don't forget that it is every child's job to start growing away from parents and gaining some independence. Your preteens will begin to move in that direction by questioning the familiar—you. They start developing their own values by listening to and absorbing opinions outside the immediate family. They watch other people and begin to form their own opinions. When they question or disagree with your values, do not become upset or disheartened. The very fact that they are thinking about these principles and ideals show that you have taught them well. You have given them a solid foundation from which to grow. After all, if they had not absorbed your standards over their first decade of life, they would be entering adolescence from soft, shaky ground. On the other hand, if they have soaked up your values but never question them, you would have unthinking, passive children. So when they challenge you and express differences of opinion, pat yourself on the back for having guided them well to a normal stepping stone toward independence.

Also consider this: Throughout adolescence—if it has not already occurred—your children will argue with you, challenge you, probably even shout "I hate you!" on heated occasions. That means it is all the more important that they have other trusted adults in their lives. Sure, it hurts when they turn on you, but it is also reassuring to know that they have a safe place to go and a responsible person to talk to when they go through rough patches with you.

Don't Leave It to Chance

You may not be able to hold tight control over the adult role models your child chooses, but you can influence positive ones. The important thing is to be alert and take an active part; do not leave it to chance.

Look around and consider which adults can reinforce the values that you hope your child will adopt and follow. The obvious ones come to mind right away: the calm, collected coach; your child's favorite uncle, aunt, or grandparent; the youth leader at your religious center; a scout leader; the nurse or physician who has taken a personal interest in your child; admired teachers; reliable neighbors; and certain friends' parents. You probably know a lot of adults who could be strong role models and provide supportive relationships, but many of us take these people for granted.

As difficult as it may be for you, these relationships have the most effect when your child views them as independent of parents. In other words, don't expect your son or daughter to report back to you. Kids need confidential relationships. Sometimes they use those alliances to run ideas past an adult before they come to you, the parent. Why? Because disappointing you is actually the hardest thing for them to do.

You could try gathering the courage to say to someone you select (say, your sister Betty), "You know, Betty, Nicole really adores you, and I trust your judgment with her so deeply. I would really appreciate it if you could begin spending more time with her so your relationship could grow even closer. What's nice is that you never have to discipline her, so she'll just keep seeing you as her Awesome Aunt. I want you to be there for her if she ever has something private to talk about and doesn't feel comfortable coming to me. You have my trust. Just guide her and give her privacy if she asks for it. Of course, I know that if she were ever in real, immediate danger, you would guide her to let me help."

Grandparents naturally fit the role of being positive influences. Isn't it one of life's great twists that the same parents who were so strict with you are so laid back with your kids? (Ah, the benefit of loving a child infinitely while having the freedom to say good-bye and go home at the end of the day.) Grandparents can give children unconditional love and plenty of harmless spoiling, so they are often the most adored adults in a child's life. Use grandparents the same way you would use Aunt Betty.

Think also of some unlikely influences, such as those people who play cameo roles in your child's life but who have a strong influence. An example:

Rodney and his school bus driver would seem to have little in common. Mr. Glenn lived in a blue-collar neighborhood and worked several jobs to support his family. Rodney lived in an upper-middle-class neighborhood and attended a private school. But Mr. Glenn often talked to the kids who sat near the front of his bus about events of the day—news about local crime, sports figures, man-bites-dog stories. If something unusual or upsetting happened in school, Mr. Glenn often put it into perspective, and the kids especially enjoyed his sense of humor.

From the bus news that Rodney brought home, his mother could tell that Mr. Glenn was opening Rodney's eyes to a wider world. She concluded that Mr. Glenn's views were interesting and his values were admirable. She encouraged Rodney's relationship with Mr. Glenn in small ways: by casually mentioning something she had heard on the radio and adding, "Have you asked Mr. Glenn what he thinks about that?" and by getting a get-well card for Rodney and the other kids to send to Mr. Glenn when he was ill.

After three years of riding on Mr. Glenn's bus, Rodney went to another school. He never saw Mr. Glenn again, but the bus driver had provided a strong, commonsense role model whom Rodney remembered for years.

It is important to encourage young adolescents to develop independent, special, even confidential relationships with other trusted adults. They might have a Mr. Glenn in their lives or a coach or teacher in whom they can confide when they are in trouble, so look around for adults who can offer your preteen a relationship that is independent of yours.

You can begin by identifying particular adults whom your child likes, feels comfortable with, and admires—someone your child thinks is more "with it" than you are! Allow it to happen as naturally as possible. Let them spend time together. Let other adults be the cool ones. And do not expect them to report back to you; just trust them.

You cannot force such a relationship, but you can foster it, just as you encouraged friendships with certain peers. You may want to discuss your plan specifically with those adults. Tell them that you would like them to play an active role in your child's life. Here are two brief hints to make your plan work effectively:

1. Do not tell your child of your plan. If he discovers that you are deliberately setting up a relationship, he may distrust the other adult or see him or her as the enemy or spy.

2. Allow the relationship to begin at as early an age as possible so that it becomes well-grounded. The earlier it takes root, the stronger it will become as your child's challenges grow during adolescence.

When There Is a Specific Problem

Earlier in this chapter we gave the example of a group of parents who got together when they began to see problems on the horizon for their preteen daughters. In that case, the parents formed an alliance among themselves. The same strategy can be altered a bit when you encounter problems; you can go to a

trusted adult who knows or works with a group of kids. Here's
a true example:

Like many parents across the country, several Philadelphia
families were agitated to discover that their preteen sons were
surfing the Internet to find pornographic sites. The boys
swapped information about these sites with each other and clev-
erly circumvented parents' attempts to limit their Internet
access. Individually, the parents felt they were getting nowhere
with their sons. The boys denied the charges or promised they
would stop. Yet it continued behind their parents' backs, so the
adults banded together to find a solution.

Several of the boys belonged to a scout troop whose 30-
year-old leader sported a shaved head and an earring and
worked in the computer industry. When the parents approached
him with their dilemma, they said, "Our sons look up to you.
They think we are stupid old parents, but they think you're terrific. Maybe you can speak to them about this problem."

When the scout leader began talking with the boys, who
ranged from ages ten to thirteen, they began to giggle. Some
denied that they participated in any web surfing activity. Others opened up and said they did it not so much for the content but to be able to go in to school the next day and brag to
their friends that they had found a particularly gross porno
website.

The scout leader explains, "I didn't try to scare them or lecture them because that would only make them want to do it
more behind their parents' backs. But I took the approach of
saying, 'This is serious stuff. There are people putting this
pornography out there for little kids to see. It's not cool to play
their game.'" He and the parents found that most of the boys
lost interest and stopped.

When you are looking for another adult to play a role in your child's life, you may find one very close by, perhaps one of your best friends. In *I Know Just What You Mean: The Power of Friendship in Women's Lives*, authors Ellen Goodman and Patricia O'Brien relate how two close friends, Linda and Melba, embraced and supported each other's daughters:

> How many times have they been each other's child-rearing adviser and expert? When Linda found herself embroiled in a fight with her preadolescent daughter over whether she could wear a bra, it was Melba who counseled, "For God's sake, buy the child a bra, what do you care?" and, years later, ran interference for the girl when Linda complained that the bra strap was showing under her daughter's tank top. And when Melba is too strict with her daughter, it's Linda who takes Ashley's side. No, it isn't just that they take care of each other's children, they point out, they feel each one's child is their own.

On my own block I have witnessed the development of some of the finest young people. The day we moved in I was still painting a room at midnight. Outside in the street, I noticed several fifteen- and sixteen-year-olds playing Frisbee in absolute silence so they would not disturb sleeping neighbors. I became intrigued by this group of young people who seemed so comfortable in their role as teenagers and so deeply respectful of adults. I later learned that their parents had formed an active alliance when the group was in late childhood. The teens knew that many of the adults on the street were always watching out for them and were available to help them work through any crisis. Now in their early twenties, whenever they come home from college they go house to house to visit their neighborhood "aunts" and "uncles."

Community Resources

If you have difficulty finding an adult with whom your child could develop a good relationship, someone whom your child already knows and likes, you may want to turn to resources in your community. Ask at your place of worship, the local school, youth groups, or sports associations about getting your children involved in activities where they will meet good adult role models. Or ask parents of your children's friends whom they would suggest. Perhaps the parent who wins the "coolest" award would be willing to develop a closer relationship with your child.

Teach One, Reach Another

As you round out a rich, supportive environment to reinforce positive behaviors, do not forget the people whom children most admire. Consider this:

What does a ten-year-old want to be? A twelve-year-old.

What does a twelve-year-old want to be? A fifteen-year-old.

Most children look up to kids who are somewhat older—a big sister, an older cousin, the high school athlete or musician who lives down the street.

As thirteen-year-old Ari put it, "I have a couple of smaller cousins who look up to me. Like, when they come over and I sit down, they'll sit exactly the same way I do. They'll do exactly what I do. It's a big responsibility 'cause I don't want to do something they'll copy that they shouldn't do."

Or as sixteen-year-old Trevor said, "Older brothers and sisters can have a positive influence because younger kids look up to them and see them almost as heroes."

Parents can capitalize on this reality by encouraging pre-teens to spend time and model themselves after responsible older teens. And this has a double bonus: not only will there be one more trusted person in your child's life, but the older teen will also benefit greatly by being respected and influential.

You might identify an older adolescent such as one of your older children, a neighbor, a relative, a babysitter, a son or daughter of one of your friends. Take him aside and say something like this:

"You know, Joseph, I've noticed that you're really growing up. I remember when you used to get into some trouble a while back, but I see that you have become a lot more responsible and mature. I'd like you to be a role model for my son. You know, just keep an eye out for him, talk to him from time to time, make sure he's not getting into any trouble. He looks up to you, and I know he will listen to you."

This expression of confidence in the older teen can make him feel proud and powerful. And if he does take on a big-brother role, your child will enjoy a positive yet not controlling relationship.

Caution: Just as you did not let your child know that you were deliberately staging relationships with other adults, do not let on that you have selected Cool Cousin to be a teenage role model or he will become suspect!

Can you guarantee that the people around your child will reinforce only positive behaviors? Of course not, but you do have the power to assure that your son or daughter will engage in activities that foster constructive behaviors and will be surrounded and supported by at least a group of people likely to promote reasonable, safe choices.

8

Discipline Through Guidance, Not Punishment

The word *discipline* means "to teach" or "to guide." But it has come to take on a rather negative connotation of heavy-handed punishment. That's unfortunate. True discipline—guiding and teaching—is one of the most important responsibilities of being a parent. Your disciplinary style can promote constructive growth in your teenager, or it can have the opposite effect. The goal is to make it an important cornerstone of your strategy for reinforcing desirable behaviors.

Discipline can be a positive responsibility, one that is challenging but also can be valuable and productive. If we guide our children with a style that enhances their growing responsibility, discipline can become a beneficial experience, a way of showering children with loving attention, far more rewarding than scolding, lecturing, berating, or punishing harshly.

Discipline is not a one-way street. It is not a matter of an active parent dispensing discipline to a passive child like cough medicine on a spoon. The child is an active participant. In fact, it is usually the child who makes the first move, and for a very specific reason. Here's a key point to keep in mind:

Every child has a fundamental need to gain parents' attention. Kids crave it, need it, and thrive on it. How do they get parents' attention? Largely by doing something that merits a disciplinary response. Most kids are experts at drawing you into their circle by behaving in ways you cannot disregard. Whether they argue, whine, complain, talk back, kick their sister, slam doors, blow smoke in your face, or take the car without your permission, they produce behaviors that require you to step in with some disciplinary measure.

This can cut two ways. Your discipline may come down on the side of negative attention: punishment, yelling, scolding, bribing, threatening. Or your discipline can be so loving that it comes in the form of positive attention.

If you have been caught in a cycle of negative interactions, you know how difficult it is to break that pattern and return to the positive relationship that you desire. But it certainly can be done. Chapters 9 and 10 will offer specific strategies for positive discipline, but we first need to understand the pitfalls of negative discipline and why they occur.

Here's a short exercise: Look back over the past week and recall each time you had to step into your disciplinary role. What lit the match? Did your kids start squabbling among themselves and come running to you to solve their problem—to blame and punish one and reward the other? Did your child interrupt you repeatedly during an important phone call until you had to send her out of the room?

Now peel another layer off that onion. What do you think lurked beneath your children's actions in each case? Had they tried and failed to get your attention so they upped the ante, acted out a bit more, and finally drew your fire?

Next, try to keep a diary—written or mental, whichever works better for you—that records actions and interactions from this moment into the next week. You will begin to notice patterns, ways your children get your attention, and your typical responses. Once you are aware of the cycle, it will be easier to learn how to break it.

The Importance of Positive Attention

A primary way to break the cycle is to *replace negative attention with positive attention.* We'll discuss this in greater detail in Chapter 10, but the bottom line for now is this: catch your children being good; remark about something they did or said that pleased you. Give kids your positive attention by spending time simply having fun with them. It can be only a few minutes a day or several times a week, but focus on them as you both do something enjoyable together. You do not have to take them on an expensive vacation or spend a lot of money, but you can try to build positive attention into your daily encounters such as sharing a joke, playing games during a car ride, or singing along to the radio as you're preparing dinner.

These brief, light moments are occasions to shower your children with loving, undivided attention. They are not fix-it occasions for teaching them something or improving their math skills; instead, they are moments when parent and child connect and simply enjoy each other. During these times, the word *discipline* is the farthest thing from your mind, but you *are* disciplining—guiding, teaching—by paying loving attention to your child. This pays off, believe me, much more than negative attention because the more positive attention they receive from you, the less they feel the need to win your attention through undesirable behaviors.

Many parents strive to hand out appropriate consequences when a child misbehaves or breaks the rules. The "punishment must fit the crime" axiom works in theory and has been promoted by many parenting advisors. But it is a difficult rule to follow consistently. Sometimes it is easy, as in this fairly trivial example:

Dad is trying to prepare dinner in a crowded kitchen. He has asked Jeremy several times to stop running in and out of the kitchen with the puppy. Jeremy ignores Dad's requests and warnings until he and the dog collide, slam into the table, and send all of Dad's lasagne ingredients flying. Dad announces the consequence: Jeremy must clean up the mess and help start dinner all over again. Fair enough.

Sometimes finding an appropriate consequence is not so straightforward, as in the following example:

Lynda gets home forty-five minutes after her curfew. Her parents are worried and angry. She tiptoes in. They confront her. She says, "I couldn't help it. I asked my friends to leave earlier, but Rebecca, the only one who drives, wasn't ready. Then she had to drop off Tamika and Will first." Her parents find it hard to be sure that the punishment fits the crime for two reasons: First, it is quite difficult to figure out what would be a fair, equal consequence for the real "crime" of being forty-five minutes late. Second, her parents may not be totally rational at the moment because they've become worried and angry while waiting for her return.

Lynda's parents are in a dilemma: They want her to face an appropriate consequence, but what would a reasonable one be? If they ground her for two weeks, she will feel like a victim. She will only be angry at them or wallow in the "It's Rebecca's fault" excuse and believe that she is being punished too harshly for a situation she could not control. When kids are put in a position where they feel like victims, we lose the opportunity to teach the desired lesson—in this case, that Lynda should have taken responsibility for getting home on time. She could have asked Rebecca when she was leaving, if she could drive her home by her curfew, and if not, Lynda could have found another ride or called home for her parents to pick her up.

Our goal is to teach the desired lesson, but our stress level prohibits us from calmly stating the points we want to make. Instead, we pour our energy into coming up with The Punishment. (The next chapter will explain how to lay out consequences in advance so that they are understood and easily implemented, rather than construct them on the spot or after the fact.)

The diagram on page 158 illustrates several directions that disciplinary action takes in a typical family. It begins when Mom or Dad states a request or command ("You must . . ."). At the first statement, the child responds either by obeying, and life rolls along happily, or deciding not to obey. That noncompliance may take the form of ignoring the parent's warnings and commands, trying to stall and avoid them, or defying them outright ("No, I won't, can't . . .").

If it takes that direction, the parent repeats the command; the child responds with negative words or inaction, and the cycle repeats itself three to seven times. Each parent has a personal threshold for the number of repeated requests he or she is willing to make. And the child knows that threshold as well

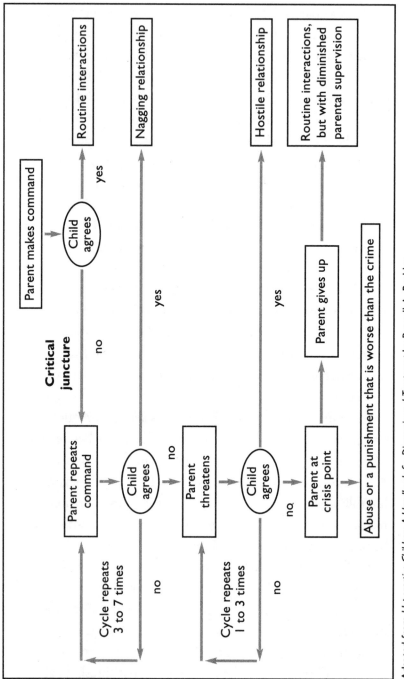

Critical juncture

Parent makes command → Child agrees
- yes → Routine interactions
- no → Parent repeats command

Parent repeats command → Child agrees
- yes → Nagging relationship
- no → Parent threatens

Cycle repeats 3 to 7 times

Parent threatens → Child agrees
- yes → Hostile relationship
- no → Parent at crisis point

Cycle repeats 1 to 3 times

Parent at crisis point → Parent gives up → Routine interactions, but with diminished parental supervision

→ Abuse or a punishment that is worse than the crime

Adapted from *Hyperactive Children: A Handbook for Diagnosis and Treatment* by Russell A. Berkley.

as he knows his own name. He knows just how far to push the limit of refusals. After all, the longer he can prolong this dance, the more attention he gets from his parents.

At some point he makes a choice, usually after he has used up all the repeat commands allotted in his household. He then complies with the request and the conflict ends. But if their interactions consistently follow this pattern, this boy and his parents are stuck in a nagging relationship.

If he has not received enough attention by this point, he will still refuse to give in and comply. Then it moves a notch higher: Mom or Dad threatens ("If you don't, I'll . . ."). The threat does not work. The child either thinks it is a bluff, does not care, or is willing to gamble that Mom and Dad will not follow through on the threat. Whatever the reason, the child still has his parents on the ropes. He is maximizing their attention, even if in the negative form of threatening. If the child buys into the threat and complies, Mom and Dad's attention would go away. So what's the incentive?

At the least he will get the most attention possible. He knows his parent's pattern. If Mom threatens only once before the consequence, he will decide whether or not to give in then. If Mom threatens three times, you can be sure he will use the full quota. Then he may cave when he has maximized Mom's attention. But if threatening has become the pattern, parent and child are mired in an unnecessarily hostile relationship.

What if the child does not give in at the final threat? The interaction is then pushed to the next higher level: now the parents are at a crisis point; they are angry that the child not only is disobeying the original command but has become even more defiant. At this critical point, Mom and Dad seem to have only lose-lose options. They can follow through on the threat. But since threats are usually made when parents are in the throes of irrationality, the resulting punishment is usually far worse than the original crime. Parents tend to increase the punishment as the defiance or backtalk continues, while the child stays focused on the original offense. He says or thinks, "All I did was . . ." and concludes that the heightened punishment is only for the initial problem, not his ongoing disobedience. The child feels like a victim and does not learn any lesson about responsibility or problem solving.

The parents' other option is to cave in and walk away. If they choose this route, life may seem easier at first, but they have lost control. A great deal of negative attention has been wasted. The child has learned how to manipulate events to hold onto parents' attention and still win—or at least not comply with the original request. In the worst-case scenario here, delinquency can develop.

How to Avoid the Trap

The most important part of the diagram is the *critical junction* at the very beginning. If we are going to avoid the lose-lose outcome, we must not even enter these negative cycles. Avoid them like Dante's circles of Hell because they will only suck you into the destructive interactions that you want to minimize.

Two key points that you must make crystal clear from the outset:

1. Certain behaviors are not negotiated.

2. Consequences are immediate.

If you allow yourself and your child to move into the negative side of that critical junction, a cycle of negotiation and second chances becomes inevitable. Instead, prepare to avoid that cycle by having an arsenal of fair, consistent, expected, pre-determined consequences that will occur if your child refuses to comply with your request or behaves irresponsibly or dangerously. (More about this in Chapter 9.)

Negotiation—Never? Or in Advance?

I do not want to send the wrong message that parents should never negotiate. Learning effective negotiation skills is an important part of growing up because it allows young people to articulate and promote their points of view. These skills also can come in handy when they need to negotiate their way out of a difficult position with peers. Negotiation is meaningful for parents as well because it shows your child that you are not totally inflexible or rigid. The deciding factor is *when* to negotiate.

I advocate negotiating when it is used *preventively*. Think of negotiation as preventive medicine, if you like, to be used before a crisis erupts. For example, when you are discussing your daughter's plans for the coming weekend, it is fine to give her some room to negotiate the arrangements: where she will be going, whom she will be with, an acceptable curfew, a plan to call home and check in or make arrangement to get home on time. Young teens need to begin these give-and-take exercises on a small scale so that they can practice them and develop increased responsibility for their choices. You can practice negotiation and compromise with the less vital issues—bedtime, video selection, clothing, haircuts, phone privileges. But remember that you, the parent, set the limits. You provide the structure.

During the give-and-take of negotiations, be sure to listen actively and attentively to your child. Let her know that she is being heard, that she can trust you to listen to her viewpoint and consider it seriously, even if you do not ultimately agree with her or grant all her requests. We must build a foundation of really listening closely if preteens are to develop the trust to come to us with critical adolescent issues and problems in a few years.

The "no negotiation and no second chances" prescription should be applied to the Big Items. Those are the issues that mean the most to you and your family. They may refer to good grades, no drugs, hanging out with particular friends—they are your choice; they reflect your family's values. In other words, pick your battles. There is no need to set limits on everything, just those matters that you consider essential to your child's growing up to be safe and responsible.

The major, nonnegotiable issues should be discussed *in advance*. You need to make clear to your children that there is no flexibility about them. No drugs means NO DRUGS. It does not mean, "OK, maybe one experimental smoke." Never getting into a car with a driver who has been drinking means exactly that, not "well, he only had one beer."

Your young teen should be very clear—from the beginning — about which Big Items you feel most strongly about, the ones that are nonnegotiable and absolute. Do not simply assume that because you spelled it out once last summer, your kids understand this fully and always remember it. Go over your priorities from time to time to remind and clarify in advance. This should not be a lecture. It can be done at leisurely times when things are calm—not in the heat of a crisis.

Saving Face

A lot of families tell me that they place a high priority on allowing children to maintain their dignity and sense of self. This disciplinary style means not criticizing or embarrassing children in front of others, particularly their friends or significant adults. These parents find that an effective disciplinary strategy is to have a private discussion with the child about the situation, its repercussions, and ways to prevent repetition in the future.

If a situation flares up in a public setting, they remove themselves and take the child aside before starting a quiet, private discussion. This worthwhile approach takes time, patience, and a measure of restraint. It is natural to blurt out a critical comment when your son has said something rude in public or your daughter has hurt someone's feelings. Your instinct is to put a lid on the situation at once, to exert some damage control. But preteens and adolescents are supersensitive about being corrected, criticized, or reprimanded by parents in the presence of other people.

If you can take them aside and speak to them privately, they will not feel embarrassed or on the spot. Their tender pride will not be shattered. And when they are allowed to save face, they will be less defensive. They will not focus so much on "Why are you picking on me? Why did you have to say that in front of my friends?" They will be more receptive about seeing the situation for what it is and learning from their mistakes.

Family Meetings

The concept of a family meeting is not new or revolutionary. Many experts have advocated the idea of sitting down together to brainstorm ideas about behaviors and their consequences, to hash out a potential problem, listen to each others' viewpoints, compromise and agree on solutions that work for everyone. A lot of families use the family meeting successfully. It can be a good proactive process for everyone involved. But when family meetings fail—ending up in arguments or in a solution dictated by a parent—everybody usually throws up their hands and says, "That's a stupid idea." So the family meeting is judged ineffective and never attempted again.

That failure tends to occur when a family sets up a meeting in the face of a crisis. Somebody has *really* messed up. The family meeting is seen as a bandage, an immediate solution.

For family meetings to succeed and to become a comfortable tool for problem-solving, they should be scheduled *before* a critical issue arises. Get your kids in the habit of suggesting situations that can be discussed at the next family meeting, even if that subject has not reached the problem stage. Think of it as a brainstorming session that begins with "What if" ("What if you caught me doing . . . What if I got into trouble with . . .").

Family meetings can be occasions for pleasurable activities, discussion, and planning. When there is no emotionally hot topic sizzling on the table, kids and parents can discuss scenarios and solutions with cooler heads. Here are some guidelines to keep in mind during family meetings:

- The goal is to brainstorm misbehaviors and their consequences. Do not immediately rule out an idea; talk it over; get everyone's opinion before deciding.

- Parents are the adults here, but they should not issue edicts or threats. You want kids to become responsible problem-solvers, so encourage their input. They will be much more willing to comply if they have had a voice in these decisions.

- The consequences you agree on together must be fair and clearly spelled out ahead of time if they are to be effective.

This last point is particularly important to the bigger message that I am trying to convey throughout this book: Preteens can *begin to think about* their behavior beforehand and learn to weigh the benefits and downsides with the consequences. Discussing this in a family meeting is one more way for young people to stretch their concrete thinking toward a more abstract cause-and-effect way of weighing their world.

The United Front and Time-Out

Before we move ahead, two other aspects of discipline need to be mentioned briefly: the United Front and Time-Out. I probably should not waste ink on the United Front approach because it is so basic and oft-repeated. Yet many parents forget or overlook it: *do not let your children divide and conquer.* Every child knows the old trick: when Dad says *no*, go get Mom to say *yes* (or vice versa). Don't let them split the adults in your family. If you allow this to occur, you are setting yourselves up for disaster. If you and your partner disagree about a discipline issue—which is perfectly natural because you are two separate individuals with different experiences and opinions—discuss it privately. If your child has extracted a promise from one of you without the other's knowledge or approval, do not argue about it in front of your child. Tell your child that you both need some time to discuss the matter and will get back to the child with an answer.

When your children were younger, you probably used the tried-and-true disciplinary method—the *time-out*. When little children throw tantrums, slug their siblings, and otherwise create social unrest, many parents find it effective to pick them up and place them on a stair step, in a chair off to the side of a room, or in their bedrooms, where they are supposed to cool off, sit quietly, contemplate their transgressions, and return repentant. Time-out also gives parents the opportunity to calm down and consider how to handle or improve the situation.

Why mention this now, with your children on the cusp of adolescence? It is not realistic at this age to expect them to sit in a corner and reflect for a few minutes. But don't forget the importance of giving yourself some time out to collect yourself before issuing a consequence. (Remember, we are looking for guidance, not punishment.) Asking preteens or teenagers to take some time and space to reflect on why *you* are upset still has merit. They are capable of understanding how one person's actions or words can hurt or upset another. If you begin a statement along the lines of, "I really feel angry when . . . ," they might surprise you with insight and empathy. Don't be surprised if, rather than coming back at you with excuses or yelling, they may just have learned something on their own.

One more cautionary note about discipline: however you determine consequences and however you express your expectations and disappointments in your child's behavior, try to do so in a way that never makes her think she has made a mistake in coming to you with her problems. Even when a child makes an incredibly dumb decision or falls into a pit of trouble, a parent's reaction should send the message: "Thank you for coming to me. Even though you have behaved badly, I still love you and always will." Those statements do not invalidate disciplinary consequences, but they help to ensure that the next time your child messes up, she will feel secure enough to come to you for help rather than turn away and, perhaps, seek an inappropriate outlet for her dilemma.

If parents do not temper their disciplinary style with this message, chances are that they will be viewed by their children as autocratic parents, ones who dish out consequences and punishments so sternly that there is no invitation to discuss or forgive. In looking back at your own childhood and your parents' disciplinary style (Chapter 1), if you discovered that you do not want to be an autocratic parent, try to keep in mind this thought: "I never want to make my child regret coming to me for guidance." Even as children become full-fledged teenagers, grow taller than parents, and say they cannot wait to get away from us, we still want them to come to us for guidance. In fact, don't we always want to be there for our children, even when they are adults? That desire to protect and guide remains a fundamental part of being a parent long after the job of raising a child is over. Now is the time to set the stage for a lifetime of mutual respect. At the core of that relationship must be your child's learning during adolescence, "I never made a mistake by going to my parent."

9

Increased Independence Under Your Watchful Eye

Let's look ahead over the next decade and think about your child's increasing independence. We know that autonomy is the ultimate goal of growing up, the pot of gold at the end of the adolescent rainbow, the hallmark of adulthood. No longer dependent on parents, the child stands alone after two decades.

By ages eighteen to twenty-one most young people have formed their moral character. They know right from wrong. They still take some risks, but they are better able to judge the consequences before making choices. They are beyond parental discipline at this point in their lives.

We no longer check their homework assignments, but we hope that their intellectual worlds are still expanding. They make their own decisions about college and careers, friends and lovers. They have begun to see a larger world, one where they are not always at the center but where other people's needs are considered and respected. Now they are young adults who have moved out of their parents' homes—to return, parents hope, only temporarily. By their midtwenties, most no longer rely on their parents for financial support.

We know that a child's independence is achieved in fits and starts over a long span of years. As we look at our ten- or twelve-year-olds today, we wonder how smooth or rocky their paths to autonomy will be.

What can we do to guide them toward independence without stealing it from them along the way? It is a complex balancing act. We certainly do not toss them into an abyss of dangers and expect them to emerge safely into adulthood. And we cannot constantly hold their hands, stand by their sides, and whisper wisdom into their ears until they reach age twenty-one. (I would point out that, while age eighteen is the legal marker of adulthood, adolescence stretches closer to the early twenties for most young people in a developmental sense.)

Between those two extremes of cold-turkey independence and prolonged overprotection lies a middle road that must be highly proactive. We can guide preteens and teens toward safer, gradual independence by two simultaneous methods:

1. Give them increasing freedoms.

2. Minimize the chances that they will make unsafe decisions.

Think of this as holding two reins, one in each hand. Sometimes you will need to pull in on the left rein and let out a little slack on the right. This is a complicated dynamic, believe me, but you can do it successfully.

At the other end of those reins, children play the essential role of pulling away from you and pushing the limits set by you, school, community, and society. Young teens are also straining toward more independence at one moment and retreating from it the next. At this tender preteen time, you know from experience that kids think they are mature enough to handle anything: "I know what to do . . . You don't need to tell me that . . . I can do it myself . . . I'm not a baby, you know, so stop treating me like one."

Of course, an hour later they come to you in tears because their hearts have been broken by a so-called friend's sarcastic remark, because they were not picked for the school play or the soccer team, or because they are fearful about trying something new or going somewhere unfamiliar.

Young adolescents *must* push the limits and challenge adult rules and values. We must allow them to test us, or else we will *prevent* them from growing up. Struggling for increased freedom is the *job* of early adolescents. It is their developmental task. But this task cannot be left to chance. Parents need to participate actively in the journey toward independence by letting their children grow step-by-step along a protected path. In other words, parents provide a safety net while their young teens take tentative steps on the tightrope.

The approach that I am about to describe on the following pages is designed to let you and your preteen work together toward safe, responsible growth. This plan has two direct benefits. First, it eliminates the need for your child to rebel outwardly in those negative, destructive, hurtful ways that too often characterize a stormy adolescence. And second, it offers you clear guidelines for effective discipline.

The strategy has two essential, complementary components: *earned freedoms* and *improved communication*.

Earned Freedoms

The basic principle here is earned freedoms—with the emphasis on *earned*. Parents do not dole out privileges and freedoms as rewards or hold them over a child's head like bribes. Earned freedoms are not tools to control young teens in a tight or autocratic way. Nor are they simply given as unrestricted gifts from the goodness of a parent's heart.

Instead, children *earn* more freedoms gradually according to a plan that both of you agree upon in advance and can measure in concrete ways. You will begin this process by each stating your needs and wants in writing. Then you will discuss, negotiate, and incorporate everything into a contract that can be reevaluated periodically. Here's how it works:

Even before you bring up this subject with your child, please read over the remainder of this chapter and look at the illustration on page 173, which shows a sample of a child's and a parent's lists of wants and needs. It is important to understand the big picture as well as the specific goals and strategies before you sit down to talk with your child.

Begin with this basic foundation: at this age, your son or daughter wants more freedom and less parental control; you need to be assured that your child is safe and responsible while growing more independent of you. These two positions may seem difficult to reconcile when you begin this process so they require considerable thought and discussion up front.

From the list of wants and needs that you and your child will write down, you will jointly forge a contract that you will each sign. I suggest that you and your children agree at the outset that this is a serious document; you will put your signatures to it to signify its importance. When you begin, you may not find that it is an instantly perfect agreement, but neither of you

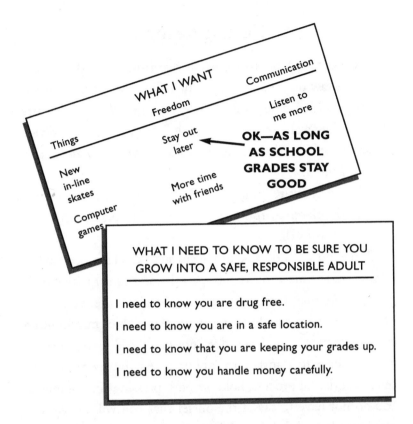

This is not a simple process, but it can be very rewarding. Your job
is to agree to as many requests as possible, but to link them to
your expectations of safe, responsible behavior.

can change or renege on it whenever you hit a bump in the
road. As part of the contract, you can agree to renegotiate it
periodically. Some families find it helpful to evaluate how it is
working every three or four months or at the beginning or end
of each season. This allows both of you to see how well it is
succeeding and whether you may need stricter safety measures.
And hopefully, you can grant more freedoms because your child
has handled current freedoms with such maturity.

Getting Ready

The negotiation process begins on two fronts. Child and parent each draw up separate lists. The child's list is titled "What I want," and the parent's is "What I need to know to be sure you grow into a safe, responsible adult." Ask your child to divide "what I want" into three column headings: *things, freedoms,* and *communication.*

They may write "things" such as a computer game, new bike, body piercing, room of my own, CD player, my own phone and so forth.

"Freedoms" tend to be privileges such as a later bedtime or curfew, more time with friends, permission to wear makeup, or going to the mall without Mom tagging along. Let your child know that these freedoms must be reasonable. Hitchhiking cross-country at age eleven does not qualify. But "reasonable" does not have to translate to "granted." As you start this contract negotiation process, hold off on expressing your opinions. You do not have to say at the outset that you will or will not grant the desired freedom. That will come later in the negotiation process.

The communication column will not become a part of your contract, per se. But it should be included as part of your child's written "want list" because good, respectful two-way communication between child and parents is essential to making the journey toward safer and greater independence a reality. Any item that your child writes down under the *communication* heading should include concrete suggestions for improved parent-child communication, such as being listened to, hearing my side of the story, not being interrupted. We will discuss the communication part of this strategy in more detail a little later in this chapter.

Parents' Need to Know List

I suggest that you call your list "What I need to know to be sure you grow into a safe, responsible adult," but that is not carved in stone. Feel free to add words like "kind," "understanding," "considerate," or whatever adjectives suit your desires and hopes for your children to become as adults.

The element of surprise is important here. However you title your page, it should be in sharp contrast to what your children would expect you to write. Their fantasy is that you will head your list "What I need to control you" or "How I can ruin my child's life." That's how most kids experience parental discipline or rules—as the harsh parental drive to squash freedom and individuality. This negotiating session can serve as a pleasant periodic reminder to your child that your motivations are actually somewhat noble and benevolent. It may just set the stage for better communication between you.

When you write down your needs, use simple phrases to describe the basic requirements needed to be certain that your child is headed in a safe, responsible direction. This is not an occasion to state, "I need you to get into a top college, to become a Nobel prize winner, or to get a billion dollar deal from an NBA team."

Many parents have written statements like these:

I need to know that you are in a safe place.
I need to know you're with dependable friends.
I need to know that you are free of drugs.
I need to know you understand that money must be earned (that you respect the value of money, or whatever way you wish to state your values).
I need to know that you are keeping up with your school-

work (are working to get decent grades, or whatever wording would apply to your child's situation).

Warning: Avoid petty or judgmental statements like "I need to know you won't wear grungy clothes because you'll look messy." Stick to subjects that are really meaningful in the long run, things that will matter over time in supporting your child's progress toward greater responsibility and maturity.

Another key ingredient is to select only items that you can measure and verify. You can monitor school grades, for example, so a statement such as "I need to know that you're keeping up your grades" can be clearly understood and gauged. Similarly, you can monitor the amount of time your children spend watching television, playing video games, or using the computer for nonschool purposes. If their homework is suffering as a result, you again have a verifiable standard: you can count the number of hours spent on schoolwork and the number of hours spent on television and other amusements.

Another example: If you want your children to appreciate the value of earning money (as opposed to expecting parental handouts), you can verify whether or not they do jobs around the house, mow lawns, take care of neighbors' pets, or baby-sit.

On the other hand, if you write "I need to know you will never use foul language," you will never be able to verify that—unless you stoop to planting a bug in their backpacks or wiretap their phone conversations. Leave unmeasurable things like that out of the contract.

You may wonder whether and how you can verify "I need you to be drug free." On page 199 the "check-in rule" is described as one way to monitor possible drug use. If you want to be sure that your children are hanging out with "dependable friends," you may not always be able to verify that need with hard evidence. But you will know from their behaviors—whether they come home on time, for example. You may want to review Chapter 7 for the importance of getting to know your children's friends and ways to do so.

Let the Negotiations Begin

When you and your child are ready to sit down and write out your lists, here are three guidelines to keep in mind:

1. These lists will form the basis for a negotiation process. The contract that you and your children will draw up and sign is based on their wants and your needs. Tradeoffs will be involved. Your children will earn certain things on their "wants" lists when they meet some of your "needs." Be sure that both lists are as clear and explicit as possible and that both of you understand them in the same way.

2. Try to agree with as many of your children's requests as are reasonably possible, but link them to your expectations of their safe, responsible behavior. For instance, if a $100 pair of in-line skates is on your child's list of "things" and "I need to know you appreciate the value of money" is on your list, you can link the two in your contract by agreeing that your child will earn the skates when he performs $100 worth of jobs around the house. In deciding on those jobs and their value, the chances of success will be greater if you seek your child's input rather than dictating them yourself.

Another example: If your child seeks "more time with friends," you can connect that "want" to your requirement "I need to know you are in a safe location" by negotiating an agreement that your child will telephone you at a designated time to report where she is and which friends are with her.

In other words, for the contract to succeed, the items on your child's list should be coupled with your expectations.

3. Tell your child if you think a request is too bold, impractical, or unreasonable. If he wants no curfew at all, for example, say that is unacceptable. Then negotiate an hour that is reasonable and satisfactory to both of you. You might begin by finding out what curfews his friends or classmates have.

The "Communication" Column

The third column on the child's list is *not* a collection of bargainable "wants." Unlike *things* and *freedoms*, the requests in this column are not negotiated or traded for progress toward greater responsibility. Obviously, you do not "listen to me more" in exchange for your child's keeping his grades up or staying drug free. But I suggest including the *communication* section on the child's "what I want" sheet because those items serve as ongoing reminders to be alert to the importance of continually improving communication between you.

You probably will not be surprised by the items that your child writes down under *things* and *freedoms*, but you may be quite surprised by what appears under the *communication* heading. From my experience with adolescents, I have found that their major and most frequent complaint is the feeling that the adults in their lives are not listening to them. On those rare occasions when they do get into a serious conversation with Mom or Dad, many kids say that their thoughts are interrupted by parents who jump in with comments and advice. Parents do not mean to squash communication. This happens unintentionally as soon as parents become alarmed by something a child discloses. It is a natural impulse, but parents need to be aware of it and stop themselves.

I cannot emphasize strongly enough that *failure to listen to your kids* creates a vicious cycle. Whenever a parent interrupts with a judgmental comment or piece of advice, no matter how wise it may be, a child feels he is not being heard. And if he is not being heard, he is not understood. Is it any wonder that young teens lash back with hostile remarks or storm out of the room? Parents then complain, "I get no respect." Well, it is no mystery. *Young people do not listen to adults who do not listen to them.*

The only way to break this pattern is to listen attentively without interruption and without passing judgment. Hear them out. Encourage them to keep talking by uttering short, reassuring comments like, "ummm, hmmm . . . yes, I see . . . please go on . . ." Empathize with them when they are anxious, angry, or upset by reflecting their emotions with short, supportive statements, such as "I see how that's annoying . . . You sound pretty angry . . . No wonder you are worried." Do not minimize or try to talk them out of their feelings. Do not hand them pat solutions. Empathy is the key to better communication.

You do not have to agree with all their views, but give young people the opportunity to express themselves as fully as they can. If you do not create an atmosphere where your children believe that they can always come to you and say anything that is on their mind, they will shut down. The door of communication will slam shut. They will not talk to you or listen to you if they believe you are not listening to them.

Consider carefully whatever your children write under the *communication* heading of their "What I want" part of the contract. Use their requests to open a genuine, nonjudgmental conversation about how your family could benefit by improved all-around communication.

Write the Contract

If you are at all hesitant about starting this earned-freedoms process, take heart from young people who have done it with their parents. As one thirteen-year-old told me, "When you put your ideas together, and write them down, you both get a say."

After you and your child have written down your respective "What I want" and "What I need to know . . ." lists, review and discuss the items thoroughly. Make sure you have been clear, specific, and concrete. Do not operate on assumptions.

Now both of you are ready to negotiate your contract for earned freedoms. You may not want to create this contract all in one sitting. In fact, it may be more successful if you take several days to think and talk about each item.

The contract should make clear exactly which *things* and *freedoms* are linked with particular expectations. That will make discipline far easier. Some examples: your son may travel some distance into the city or to a suburban mall by public transportation if he consistently calls home after his arrival and returns by his curfew; your daughter may be allowed to stay out until 11 P.M. if her homework is completed satisfactorily before she goes out, if you know where she is, and if she checks in with you when she comes home.

However you hammer out the contract, always link the earned freedoms to your expectations for responsibility and safety. If you begin this practice early, your children will be excited to demonstrate positive behaviors because they will know that you want to trust them and that all they need to do to earn even more freedoms is to continue maintaining your trust by complying with your expectations.

After you have written the contract down on paper and have gone over it carefully, you and your child should feel satisfied and be eager to sign. But one or both of you may eventually discover that a few of the items are not clear enough, that something has been omitted, or that one of the provisions is not working as you had expected. But remember the ground rule: the contact should be evaluated and renegotiated every few months to allow for more movement toward independence. Do not, however, try to tinker with any item whenever a problem pops up. Stick to your agreement.

Tying In Discipline

When children break some provision of the contract, the consequence is crystal clear: they lose the associated privilege or freedom. This is a direct, precisely defined way to discipline. Preteens and teens cannot claim, "I didn't know the rules" because they helped make them. They can re-earn the privilege or freedom the next time the contract is reevaluated and updated in three to four months.

This is a good time to look again at the diagram in Chapter 8 where discipline was discussed. The "critical juncture" point is usually where parents enter into a cycle of second chances, repeated commands, and inappropriate or no consequences. But once you have a written earned freedoms agreement in place and a child breaks the rules, the parent's response is predetermined. The consequence is clear: the linked freedom or privilege is lost. There is no need for a parent to become irrational, dwell on punishments, or repeat endless commands and threats; the cycle is broken.

Let's look at Lynda's parents again (see page 156) to see how their situation might have been improved by linking discipline to an earned freedoms contract. They were struggling to find a reasonable response to their daughter's coming home forty-five minutes late. If they greeted Lynda with anger, their rage may have prevented them from teaching a valuable lesson. Their punishment might have made Lynda feel victimized and thereby miss the essential problem: how she could have found her way home safely and on time. But if the family had an earned freedoms agreement already in place, her parents could have simply and calmly said, "We agreed in our current contract that you could stay out until 10:30 P.M. Because you were unable to follow through on this expectation, you will lose this privilege. When we made our earlier contract, you did a great job not coming in later than the 10 P.M. curfew we agreed to then. That will be your curfew again. If you do well with that 10 P.M. curfew, then the next time we sit down to review our contract, your curfew will be returned to where it was today. You know, Lynda, we love you so much and we're so glad to have you home safely. Go to bed. Tomorrow we'll talk about what went wrong tonight that kept you from getting home on time, unless, of course, you want to talk about anything now."

Lynda's family spent two minutes on discipline and did not get trapped in a nagging or hostile relationship. While Lynda is still likely to complain about moving backward in her earned freedoms, she knows the rules are fair because she was involved in making them.

This method has three key ingredients that ensure fair discipline: it is predetermined, consistent, and expected. And that's why it works.

Let's go a bit further and assume that you have worked hard to put into place all the techniques suggested in these pages. Ever since your child was ten or eleven, you have been using choreographed conversations instead of lectures; you have linked appropriate freedoms and limits; you have done role-plays; and you have taught refusal skills and positive coping skills. But occasionally you and your child hit a brick wall. Your child may get into trouble or your new techniques do not seem to work. A natural reaction would be to punish by lowering the boom with lots of restrictions, but you know that such action could push the child further away and provoke rebellion.

When this happens, you do not have to fall into the old negative cycle of commands, threats, and repeated commands. Instead, you can use the earned freedoms contract in a remedial way to repair the damage, get back on track, and give each other an opportunity to rebuild trust. (If you are reading this when your child is already fourteen or older and you have not yet used any of these approaches, but you need to rebuild trust with your child, this is a good place to begin using a contract.) Let's look at one family's situation.

Daniel and his parents had been at odds for several weeks about two issues: his use of the computer and staying out late. His parents thought he was spending too much time at the computer. They questioned him about what he was doing on-line and why he was staying out later and later. He argued that they were being too strict and intrusive.

The conflict came to a head when his father walked into Daniel's room, looked at the computer, and saw a log of the

websites that his son had visited recently. Dad discovered information that alarmed him: sites that showed kids how to make
homemade drugs and others that were violent, crude, and
insulting to women.

When his parents asked Daniel about these sites, he assured
them that he had never tried to make drugs or use them. A
friend had just told him about that site and Daniel wanted to
be able to say he had looked at it. His parents had no reason
to doubt him and had never seen any evidence that their son
might have tried drugs. But they were concerned about his
visiting a variety of pornographic sites, so they called me for
an appointment.

They dragged Daniel, silent and somewhat sulky, to my
office. "Is this abnormal?" they asked. I reassured them that
curiosity about sex was normal in adolescence but that some
Internet sites do not support healthy development. I recom-
mended a few books that explain sexuality in positive, normal
ways. Then I talked to Daniel alone for a while and learned that
he felt tortured by his parents. He said they didn't trust him,
and he was beginning to rebel by staying out later than they
liked.

When I talked with his parents, they said their first impulse
was to ground Daniel and take away the computer. But as they
thought about it, they recognized that their son was actually
gifted at computer technology and needed it for schoolwork. If
they did take the computer away, they knew that Daniel would
only log on at a friend's house or at the library.

I showed the three of them how a contract could improve
the situation and rebuild their trust in each other. They went
home, sat down together, and expressed their mutual concerns.
The parents said that they did not want to unplug the computer

altogether because they knew it was important to his school-work and his future, but they wanted to restrict its use.

Under their list of "needs," they described their need to know that Daniel was using the computer responsibly (i.e., not accessing inappropriate sites or chat rooms) and that he was not spending so much time on the computer that his sleep, school-work, or social life was suffering. They also needed to know he would come home on time. On his "wants" list, Daniel included computer availability to contact friends through E-mail and do school assignments, as well as some measure of privacy (i.e., his parents would not constantly look over his shoulder to see what was on the monitor).

In the negotiation process, his parents offered Daniel a choice: either the computer would be moved out of his room to a more open space, such as the family room, or if he wanted to keep it in his room, his parents would get special features, such as one that shuts down the account at 11 P.M., or they would check the computer's history files, which automatically record the last twenty-five Web addresses visited by his browser.

When the family came back to see me a few months later, I learned that Daniel had been keeping up his end of the con-tract. He had been using the computer responsibly, followed the check-in rule, and earned a later curfew and more time with friends. Most important, he was enjoying his parent's trust and felt he had a lot to lose if he rebelled any more.

In the ideal world, earned freedoms contracts *prevent prob-lems* and *build responsibility*. Yet when families do run into dif-ficulties, the same technique can be used to remedy an ongoing problem. Keep the success of Daniel's experience in mind as your child moves through adolescence and your family inevitably encounters situations that require some repair.

A Brief Review

Offering and earning freedoms through a contract like the one you are about to construct is a challenge for parents and young teenagers. If you each put serious effort and thought into it, you will achieve two important goals that both parents and children desire:

1. Your children will not see you as a controlling parent, but one who listens and respects them.

2. You will see them grow as responsible young people who earn freedoms and privileges gradually—as they become ready—and in a safe environment.

This is not a simple process. And we cannot be naive enough to think it will work in every situation. If a young person really messes up—steals a car, for example—much more serious restrictions are necessary than recalling a few earned freedoms and privileges. But for the majority of everyday interactions, a contract for earned freedoms can be very rewarding. If you hit a snag as you are working out the contract, do not get discouraged. Keep at it and try to be flexible.

10

More Attention, Less Discipline

Has your preteen started demanding more of your attention lately? Getting in your face? Pouting, whining, nagging, trying to provoke some reaction from you? "Didn't we get past the Terrible Twos?" you may have asked yourself.

If your preteen seems to spiral downward a decade, like Alice falling into not-so-Wonderful-land, you are not imagining things. You are not really trapped in a time warp. The Terrible Twos have not returned to haunt you. But in many developmental ways, children on the brink of adolescence often do behave like toddlers, challenging you and yanking you, almost physically, into their orbit.

Although this behavior is not unusual, it can be annoying and even harmful to family relationships if we allow it to go unchecked. "But why," you wonder, "are they doing this? Just to get a rise out of me?" That's just about right.

Children of all ages want their parents' love and attention. At this age in particular, they tend to get our attention by acting in ways that we cannot ignore, ways that demand some sort of disciplinary response. Usually those are negative behaviors, so we react by reprimanding the child: "Where did you learn that kind of language—don't ever say that again in this house! . . . I'm not going to spend another dollar on clothes if you insist on dressing that way! . . . Turn down that disgusting music! . . . I don't want you hanging out with kids who are a bad influence! . . . Get off the phone right this minute!"

You may not think that children *want* us to criticize or scold them with these negative responses, but they do provoke the reaction they desire—our attention. Negative attention, yes, but attention all the same. And any attention convinces them that parents care about them.

But the problem is that once parents are sucked into this cycle of paying negative attention, it becomes habitual. It wears us out. We lose the energy to break the pattern, and we give a knee-jerk reaction: "No . . . Stop! . . . Go to your room! . . . You're grounded . . . No allowance for two weeks . . ."

Children do not enjoy being on the receiving end of these contentious comments and punishments, but they continue to feed the provoke/react habit because it wins parental attention. At the same time, parents feel as though they are undergoing a slow water torture, drip by negative drip. They give in or lash back, but they do not break the pattern.

A Better Alternative

The cycle of negative attention can be broken and a better one created with a little thought and careful planning. Here is the key: *flood your child with positive attention.* This is not an invitation to spoil your children, to cave in to their every demand, to be a wimp, or to spend all your retirement savings on them. You will still need to guide, teach, set limits, and hand out appropriate consequences for breaking the rules. But this new strategy involves giving them so much love and attention *in advance* that they will feel less need to win your attention by irritating or harmful behaviors.

This is a good time to flip back to the diagram in Chapter 8. Look at the critical juncture point near the beginning of the cycle and imagine how different the parent-child relationship would be if positive attention has been showered on the child. Wouldn't he or she have much less reason to move in the contrary direction of defiance, reprimands, threats, repeated commands, and so forth?

You may be thinking, "Oh, right! My child and I are already so deep into this misbehave-reprimand cycle that a little positive attention can't possibly help." No, positive attention is not a quick fix. It is not as easy or foolproof as it may sound at first. But do not give up before you begin.

This approach is tied directly to what we have discussed about discipline. The more you give your child positive attention, the less you will need to use consequences and revoke privileges. The more positive attention you give, the less likely you will be caught up in the fruitless command-nag-threaten-command-again-and-again cycle that is illustrated on page 158. And positive attention also reinforces those constructive behaviors and more mature decisions that your child makes on the path toward increased responsibility and independence.

You will have to work at this new approach by thinking ahead to break the destructive cycle and replace it with constructive attention. Paying more positive attention is not guaranteed to change your relationship with your child overnight, or even by next month. It is a gradual process, but you will reap the rewards. Here are the rules to follow.

Catch Them Being Good

This phrase has often been used in the context of parenting younger children. The idea is to keep an eye out for desirable behaviors and reinforce them by consistent praise rather than focus on undesirable behaviors and reinforce them negatively through scolding, punishing, and reprimanding. You may have used this *positive reinforcement* approach when your preteen was much younger but have forgotten about it in recent years. Well, it can still work if you update your approach a bit!

Many parents are surprised to discover that negative behaviors diminish or melt away because children strive to please them. With very young children, this can occur quite simply. Example: Three-year-old Tameka balks at brushing her teeth each night. She continues to refuse and whine as long as Mom and Dad make a big deal of the issue. Then they back off for a few nights. They do not even utter the words *teeth* or *brush*. A few days later, they leave a brand new, hot pink toothbrush on the edge of the bathroom sink, but they say nothing about it. Tameka finds it, picks it up, squirts two tablespoons of toothpaste all over it, and brushes. When she says good-night, Mom and Dad tell her how shiny her teeth look. They praise her for "brushing like a big girl, all by herself." Over the next week, they reinforce Tameka's efforts by continuing to praise her. They gradually diminish their attention to toothbrushing, though, because they do not want to overdramatize the issue. Problem solved. The nightly fight about toothbrushing is finally over. From this single experience, Tameka's parents learned the value of giving her lots of attention to reinforce many of her other admirable behaviors that they had previously not noticed. Now they make a regular habit of "catching her being good."

With preteens and adolescents, of course, this strategy requires a bit more sophistication than buying a new toothbrush, but they still love to win your positive attention and praise. They do not have to make the honor roll, sell the most Girl Scout cookies, win a starring role in the school play, or be the best athlete to win your praise. Paying attention—catching them "being good"—can apply to scores of other, smaller scale occasions every day if we keep our antennae tuned. Examples:

Showing kindness to a younger sibling: "That was very thoughtful of you to help Willis when he got stuck on his math homework."

Expressing an interesting thought: "Umm, I never thought about it that way. I'm glad you pointed that out to me."

Helping without being asked: "Thanks for carrying in those heavy grocery bags. My aching back and I really appreciate it."

Showing respect or caring for others: "I'm sure that older gentleman appreciated it when you held the door open for him."

Sticking with a difficult task: "I noticed how much time you spent practicing your music this week. Your teacher must have given you a lot of work, and I'm proud of you for sticking with it."

Coping with problems: "That classmate's teasing must have been really annoying, but you handled it so well that you let her know she couldn't get to you."

In the course of any given day, there are probably ten to twenty little acts or remarks that deserve your attention and praise. Some may seem so insignificant—perhaps your child voluntarily turned down the TV volume when you were talking on the phone—that you may not even notice. Or if you do observe it, you may not bother to express your appreciation and admiration out loud. Start looking for these minor occasions and point them out to your child: "Thanks for hanging up those wet towels . . . That was a really funny joke—I love your sense of humor . . . I appreciate it a lot when you make your own lunch because it saves me time."

Of course, there *is* overkill. If you start praising your children every time they comb their hair, finish the food on their plates, or simply breathe, they will probably think you have gone off the deep end. Be selective and genuine, and do not lay it on too thickly. You may want to begin gradually and ease into this new approach. Expect them to say something along these lines: "Gee, Dad (or Mom), what's the matter with you? You're talking different."

If they do question the change in your words or motives, why not be up front with them and say something like, "Well, yes, but I recently realized that I wasn't paying enough attention to all the good stuff you do. I haven't been telling you often enough how proud I am of you and how happy you make me."

Be on the lookout for the small but constructive things they do and say each day, and let them know that you *notice* and *appreciate* them. After all, your children crave your attention.

They need to know that you notice them. How else do they know that you love them?

Create Special Times

Parents sometimes assume that they need to spend *less* time together as a family when their nine- to fourteen-year-old children are branching out with new friends and more away-from-home activities. Even when they do have a little "free" time, many parents presume that their kids would prefer to be with friends, so parents do not make an effort to share an activity or even take a walk with their preteens. This is a mistake—preteens need to spend *more* time with their parents, not less. Our time is a gift to them—a gift of our attention, an expression of our love and concern.

There is no magic quota for an exact number of minutes or hours, but kids this age need time with parents on a routine basis if they are to grow up safely and responsibly. Sure, they will want to spend more time with friends. They need to do that. Do not feel hurt when they tell you they would rather be at the mall or a movie with friends, but special time between parent and child does not have to be sacrificed in exchange. Help them schedule time for both.

Certainly it is difficult in today's hurried world to find much "family time." If there is more than one child in the family, time may be especially precious. Javier has hockey, Jamie has swimming, Louis has jazz—all on Saturday. Forget the middle of the week everyone is too exhausted from work and school.

But it is absolutely essential that parents find a way to spend regular time with preteens. You do not have to quit your job or book a two-week vacation to have so-called quality time with your children. In fact, some of those elaborately planned, horrendously expensive vacations can blow up in our faces when we overinvest emotionally and financially in turning them into perfect Kodak memories.

A more valuable, less stressful, and certainly less expensive strategy is to create frequent, small-scale snapshot times, not big panoramic extravaganzas. The key element is still attention—*positive* attention—paid to each child individually. Here are some suggestions:

• Consider what your child enjoys and build special times upon those interests. Plan excursions, events, and conversations around activities that your child likes—and that you also enjoy. If your child loves hiking and camping but you hate roughing it, you will not be able to feign pleasure when you are swatting mosquitoes in a cramped tent in the woods at midnight. Forget that and find another interest that delights both of you. Ask your child for input. Where would she like to go on Sunday afternoon? What would he like to do during next spring's school vacation? What game would she like to play after dinner?

• Make an effort to spend at least five to ten minutes every day *with each of your children alone.* This means that other siblings cannot butt in. Each child will have his or her exclusive time with Mom or Dad.

• Make "special time" a customary, high-priority part of your family routine. Those five, ten, twenty minutes of simply talking, listening to music, playing a card game, walking the dog together, or whatever you both enjoy, must be regular, predictable events that do not get shoved to the back burner. If you have to work late, are out of town, or your child has an evening activity, plan to reschedule that time on another night, but do not let it slip by.

• Special time should not be spent checking homework or doing some household chore. It should involve something pleasurable. Of course, if your child is upset by something, he may want to use this time to talk about whatever is troubling him. Take your cue from your child, but always let him know that you are available on a regular basis.

Share Time Together

You can also find opportunities when you and your child can share the day's events. This does not necessarily have to be structured or pencilled in to your schedule, but if you can manage to have a meal together, those can be the best times to talk and listen. You do not have to set a formal table with candles and linen tablecloths every night. In fact, dinnertime may be rushed or staggered depending on each family member's timetable. If you can manage to eat supper together as a family a couple of times a week, that's great. In some families, breakfast time is a good opportunity to talk about the day's expectations. Here is an example from a family in western Pennsylvania who told me of their situation and solution:

Their individual lives were spinning in so many different directions, they said, that they could have been like ships passing in the night. Parents and kids ate at different times, often standing at the kitchen counter or grabbing food as they dashed out the door. They recognized that they needed to establish some way of reconnecting. They decided, no matter how busy they are, to make a family ritual of sitting down together for dinner. Even if the food is take-out from a Chinese restaurant or a fast-food drive-through, they set the dining room table, put the food on dinner plates, and light candles. It is not formal, but their dining room has become a special place to come together on a regular basis and talk about whatever is on their minds as they share a meal. To make it work, given their crazy schedules, they get together on Sunday evenings and create a dinner schedule for the week that takes into account everyone's needs. Then they post it on the refrigerator door. While the actual dinner time may differ from day to day, the fact that they are together each night is the one constant in their hectic schedule. Their children do not consider this a required, restrictive regulation; in fact, they never want to miss a family dinner.

Riding in the car or on the bus or subway gives parents another opportunity to have a captive conversation with kids. Or waiting in the dentist's office, on the grocery checkout line, or the movie ticket line—there are countless times to strike up a brief conversation. But beware that if there are people nearby, children may be reluctant to talk as openly, or about anything private. They may be embarrassed that you are even talking to them. If that happens, just let it go. There will always be other opportunities.

The key is to be alert for occasions that spring up unexpectedly. Take advantage of those spontaneous moments to chat with your child. Here are some hints to keep the conversation going:

• Do not probe or ask for details. Your young teen will rebel—or clam up—if you ask, for example, "Which of your classmates smokes marijuana? . . . Have your friends ever talked you into shoplifting? . . . I hear that Melanie has a hot reputation. Is that true? . . ." Instead, ask more general, open-ended questions ("What was the most interesting thing that happened today? . . . What was the most boring thing?") or make short comments that invite your child to elaborate. ("I saw in the paper that there's a concert next weekend . . . The PTA says it's going to sponsor a dance next month.")

• Express interest in your child's friends' lives. Again, do not probe, but be receptive and interested when your child makes a comment like, "You won't believe what Eric did in gym class today." When they do open a conversational door, do not let it slam shut. You can encourage your child to keep talking by simply uttering brief, neutral remarks like, "Really? . . . Oh, yeah? . . . Why do you suppose that happened?"

Many preteens like to talk about their friends, but only on their terms—when they want to, not when they feel they are bring interrogated. One surefire way to cut off these conversations is to make a judgmental or critical comment about their friends. If you remark, "How could Eric be so stupid!" the conversation will screech to an abrupt halt.

• Listen. Keep your ears and mind open. Try to hear your child's whole story before offering any opinion or judgment. As we discussed earlier, children this age are particularly sensitive to "being heard." If they start to tell parents something and are interrupted by advice or criticism, they are not only likely to leave the room on the spot, but also to avoid going to their parents again when they really need to talk about something on their minds.

If your child does relate a story with some troubling ingredients, hold your tongue until the whole story is out. Then, instead of delivering a moral or judgment, it is better to reflect on the things that concern you. For example, you might say,

"That sounds like it's quite a difficult situation. Any ideas on how you could handle it best?" Pause a while and let your child think about it before saying, "Can I help?"

Above all, try to maintain some flexibility about the time you share together. It's nice to schedule dinner, an outing, or special time together, but sometimes kids need you most on their timetable, not yours. Their concerns will not always arise at times that are convenient or leisurely for you. And sometimes they will want to talk about something that is urgent to them but seems trivial to you. When your children were younger, can you recall how patient you were when they asked endless questions about every single thing or rattled on about each new realization they discovered?

One of my favorite parenting moments occurred when my then-four-year-old Talia realized that she could get the same result from two different actions. On the night of a national political convention, she and her twin sister were talking up a storm. I asked them to be quiet for "just five minutes" so I could listen to a major speech. For the first thirty seconds, they begged me to finish their stories. Then they tried "Can we talk now?" every thirty seconds. After about three minutes, Tali said, "It's really, really important. Can I just tell you quick?"

Being the strong authoritarian type, I said, "Sure, Tali."

"Daddy, did you know that when some people eat cereal and milk, they put the cereal in a bowl and pour milk on it, but other people put milk in the bowl and then put cereal on top?"

My point is twofold. First, just remember the sheer joy of watching your child make discoveries. During adolescence, their discoveries are again occurring at an undeniably rapid pace and, while they may not always tell you that they want to share them with you, they still do. Second, even though your children are as tall as adults now, try to be genuinely interested in something simply because it is important to them.

The Nightly Check-In Rule

No, this is not sleep-over camp where counselors do the bed check routine, nor is it meant to seem punitive. Establishing a nightly check-in is simply a way to assure a safe return home when your children have been out (and it helps you get a good night's sleep).

First, make sure your children understand this firm, clear rule: Come in and tell me when you get home. Even if I am asleep, wake me. Tell me you're home and safe. Talk to me for a few minutes. I will be happy to listen, no matter how sleepy I am.

Start this practice as early as possible so that it becomes an expected family rule. When children are still young enough to be put to bed, most families have an informal "good-night" ritual. Sometimes, as they get older and get ready for bed by themselves, we fall out of that habit. But it is a good practice to revive with five- to fifteen-year-olds. Even when they are old enough to be out late, you can establish the nightly check-in with a simple "come in and say good-night" habit.

Never allow any exceptions. No excuses like "I was afraid to wake you." "I was too tired." "I forgot." "I didn't feel so well." If you have made certain in advance that nightly check-in is a requirement, your child knows what to expect. Breaking this rule means losing privileges. Because this is such an effective means of monitoring your children, I strongly suggest that you always make it one of the expectations linked to your child's increasing independence (as noted in the section on earned freedoms in the previous chapter). You might express it this way: "Remember, I worry less about your staying out because I know that you will always follow our check-in rule."

The nightly check-in has two terrific benefits. For parents, it eliminates the need to wonder and worry about whether teens are on drugs or drinking. Parents will be able to determine their child's coherence much more accurately from the nightly check-in than from any drug screen or from snooping in sock drawers or from grilling a teenager.

The second benefit helps kids directly. The nightly check-in gives them a wonderful refusal skill, as explained in Chapter 5. When friends are pressuring them, they can say, "Sorry, I can't smoke that. You know my parents' stupid check-in rule. I think they actually smell my hair and my clothes when I get home and have to check in with them." or "If I'm messed up, my mom will know it and then I won't be out for a month!"

This refusal skill works effectively because it is so believable. Other kids sympathize and back off in the face of a friend's parents' "stupid check-in rule." Your child gets a breather from the peer pressure, yet does not lose face or status because you, Mom or Dad, have become the Bad Guy.

You may wonder why I have included the nightly check-in practice in a chapter about positive attention. At first, you—and more likely your children—might think it sounds a bit heavy-handed or too authoritarian. Actually it is not. When carried out in a loving spirit (as opposed to an interrogation), the regular nightly check-in is one more way of giving young teens positive attention. You are showing them that you are glad they are home safely. You want to know that they are OK. You are interested in them, their activities, their friends. You care about them. You love them.

Most nights, they will probably check in without any drama: "Hi, I'm home . . . DeeDee's dad drove us home . . . Yeah, we had fun . . . The movie was really great . . . I'm tired . . . See you in the morning." But there will be nights when they will come home worried or upset. You may smell cigarette smoke or the unequivocal aroma of marijuana. Their eyes may be wide and glassy. They may be tipsy or worse. When that happens, be grateful that they are home and that they have felt comfortable enough to come through your door for the nightly check-in. Tell them to go to sleep (or put them to bed if necessary) and tell them that you will need to talk seriously in the morning. Exploding in anger or shouting reprimands—no matter how worried they have made you—is not helpful at this highly charged moment. It also discourages them from checking in with you in the future. A better approach is to wait until the next morning to discuss their behavior and its consequences in a calmer, cooler atmosphere.

The Connection That Keeps It All Together

Do you want to prevent drug use? Raise a child who has confidence and a good sense of self-esteem? Minimize the chances that peers will have undue negative influence? Maximize the chances that your child will never have to turn to negative behaviors to reduce stress? Make discipline (in the classic sense of the word) a small part of your relationship with your child?

The bottom line is that a deep sense of *connection* between child and parent is more meaningful than anything else in terms of predicting the kind of positive outcomes we want for our children. This vital connection is about more than time; it is about genuine love and caring. Playing basketball with your son or daughter matters, but talking to them and listening to them about their concerns matters far more. Taking your child skating is wonderful, but being available when he gives you that look that says he has something on his mind is even more special.

Make no mistake about it: Your children *want* to please you. In fact, they tend to live up to—or down to—parents' expectations. This truth reminds me of a sixteen-year-old boy who rebelled in some very dangerous ways: flirting with gangs, drugs, and sex. At his core, he remained a wonderful boy who was seeking love from his parents. They were trying to rescue him from the precipice of danger, but they began to view him and treat him as a hoodlum. One day in my office, I asked his mother what she really thought of him. She said he was "big trouble."

He looked dejected and said, "If you already think I'm such big trouble, why shouldn't I be?" He was moved to tears when I helped his mother express what she really felt—that she loved him deeply, worried about him incessantly, and thought that deep down he was a kind young man struggling to live a positive life. Her words were exactly what he needed to begin the process of change. He needed her positive expectations to live up to.

Here is one more example of how kids live up to parents' expectations and when those expectations are negative, how the situation can be reversed:

Amber was doing well in school and had good friends, but she had started staying out late without explanation. Her strict parents assumed the worst—that she was meeting unsavory friends, doing drugs, having sex. She denied their accusations, but they began treating her like a Bad Girl. They forbade her from staying out after dark. When Amber came in for a routine checkup, I learned that her parents had become restrictive, though Amber was not doing the things they suspected. She felt she needed to rebel a bit against their rules.

"My parents freak out when I come home. I've never even tried drugs," Amber told me, "but I'm being treated like I do. So why shouldn't I? I'm not dating, but why not fool around if they already think I am? What's the point? Why not?"

Amber was about to make her parents' worst fears come true, so I began a choreographed conversation with her. Here are some of the prompts that I used to help her think through the situation: "What's going to happen if you do mess up, Amber? If you continue staying out late, getting too tired for school the next day, start letting your grades slip? What if you do start 'fooling around' or trying drugs? Then you'll prove your parents were right."

She nodded as she saw how these possibilities could spin out.

"So how can you win this struggle?" I asked her. "Through excellence. You know what a fine person you are, what a good student you are, that you're motivated to do well in school, that you have good friends. It's sad that your parents don't see that right now, but you can show them. Maybe it will be within a week or maybe it will take five years, but you'll be able to say to them, "You know, I was really good all along.'

"Meanwhile, let's make a contract with your parents that can rebuild their trust," I suggested.

Amber had come to believe that her parents did not love or trust her. They did love her dearly and were trying hard to protect her, but this family needed to make a much better connection. An earned freedoms contract was the way to strengthen it. Her parents wrote out their list of "needs." (To be certain that she was safe, they needed to know where she was, with whom, when and how she could return home. To be assured she would continue to do well in school, they needed to know she was spending enough time on homework and getting enough sleep.)

Amber wanted a looser rein from them. In broad terms, she wanted to know that they respected and trusted her, but for the contract she wrote specific items (a 10 P.M. curfew on school nights, an 11 P.M. curfew on weekends, for example). Under the "communications" heading, the family recognized that less interrogation, accusation, and suspicion were necessary if Amber and her parents were to rebuild trust. I described how to draft a contract, review it every three months, and use it as a basis for Amber to earn increased freedoms as she met her responsibilities. And I explained how some privileges would be revoked if she failed to meet her end of the contract. Amber and her parents went home to work on negotiating the contract. When she returned to see me several months later, Amber was less angry and was doing better in school. Her parents still worry a lot, but they have begun to see her as a successful young woman. Now Amber had something positive to live up to.

Final Thoughts

No one ever pretended that raising children is easy; it's hard work! And guiding children from age nine though adolescence is one of our biggest challenges despite its enormous rewards. With the skills and parenting styles that we have discussed in the previous ten chapters, I hope you are better prepared to support your child to become a mature, responsible young person. But even the most well-intentioned and best prepared parents sometimes may face unexpected problems.

From thousands of young patients, I have learned that adolescents in crisis literally shop for a loving, responsible adult. They shop at home, in school, in their neighborhoods, in their religious centers, and in health care settings. Over the years, I have found that simply being a caring, available adult has allowed me to influence more young lives than has any biomedical training I have received.

Young people do not ask for help directly, but they do send out subtle clues that signal they are in trouble. And they hope that an adult will be alert and wise enough to pick up on those clues. In a medical setting, usually the signals are stress-related symptoms like fatigue, headaches, dizziness, and belly pain. In the home, the signs may be acting out, fatigue, or school failure. The symptoms are real, and we must look beneath the clues for underlying causes.

I cannot end this book without spelling out some warning signs that should tip you off that it's time to consider professional involvement:

• **Changes in schoolwork.** School is the child's job, the marker of future success. If your child's grades suddenly start falling, that is a sign that something is going on. Normal ups and downs—a *B* in math one quarter, a *C+* the next, a *B−* the next—are routine. But if your child has been a consistent *B+* student in most subjects and her grades in most or all subjects suddenly drop to *C−*s or *D*s, find out what's happening.

If teachers are calling to report that your child is not completing schoolwork or is cutting class, that is another sign. Look for patterns, but do not become panicked by one or two missed assignments.

• **Withdrawal from relationships.** It is normal to start pulling away from parents at this age, but when children stop talking to you or refuse to participate in all family activities, that too is a sign that something is upsetting them.

It is *not* normal for kids to withdraw from their friends, however. If your child stops seeing friends, that is a serious sign of trouble. Or if your child suddenly dumps a group of old friends and starts hanging out with a different group, that may signal a change in behavior, such as drug or alcohol use.

• **Too much moodiness.** This is a tough one to measure because all preteens and adolescents have mood swings. But if these mood swings are so out of control that a child is threatening to hurt himself or others, that is a major warning signal.

Keep a watchful eye on your preteen's school performance, activities, moods, and friendships. And remember: *you know your child best.* If you feel any instinct in your gut that something is wrong—even if you have not actually witnessed risky behaviors or danger signs—trust your intuition.

Then take some pressure off yourself and find a responsible professional to help you evaluate your child. Do not talk yourself into believing that trouble signs will go away, or that "this is just a stage." Do not wait to seek help. You might begin by discussing the problem with your child's doctor, a trusted teacher or school counselor, or someone who knows your child well. Ask for their honest opinions about what they observe in your child's behavior and attitudes. Seek their advice.

All parents are challenged by adolescents. Expect bumps in the road over the coming years, but also remember the good news: most children weather adolescence smoothly without great storm and stress. You and your child will both survive.

My goal in writing this book has been to offer you skills and strategies to develop solid relationships with your preteens, to prevent adolescent problems, and to make your parenting style as strong and effective as possible for the sake of everyone in your family. I also want you to take away from these pages one essential truth: *you have more influence on your children than anyone else, probably more than you even realize.*

Your children love you and need your positive attention. You are in a very powerful position to help them grow up to be independent, responsible young adults. You have demonstrated your wisdom and commitment by choosing to actively improve your skills. As hard work as it is to raise teenagers in today's world, you have decided that it is well worth it. Take a deep breath and realize that if you can convey the depth of your caring to your children and learn to listen to whatever is important to them, you are almost there. If you stop lecturing, if you really think about how to help your child come to self-awareness, and if you stop thinking about discipline as punishment and begin incorporating it as active guidance, you will be well on your way toward a wonderful relationship with your child.

I have not provided you with all the answers to all the questions that may arise. No one can possibly do that for you. But I do hope that you will review these pages from time to time. When you have questions or feel stuck with a problem, talk to other parents about your concerns. There is great strength in numbers and wisdom in others' experience. And lastly, pay close attention to the wisdom of youth. Our children send us very clear messages about what they need from us. We just have to listen.

I wish you and your children the very best.

Resources

The following list of books about parenting adolescents is not intended to be comprehensive, but among a multitude of titles published each year, the following may be particularly useful:

Aftab, Parry. *The Parent's Guide to Protecting Your Children in Cyberspace.* New York: McGraw-Hill, 2000. A comprehensive guide to keeping up with the ever-changing Internet scene and its potential problems for youth.

Barkley, Russell A. *Hyperactive Children: A Handbook for Diagnosis and Treatment.* New York: Guilford Press, 1981. This out-of-print classic is from the author of *Taking Charge of ADHD.*

Bauman, Lawrence, Ph.D. *The Ten Most Troublesome Teen-Age Problems and How to Solve Them.* Secaucus, NJ: Carol Publishing Group, 1997. Suggested solutions to normal and not-so-normal problems of relationships, moods, sex, drugs, school.

Carey, William B., M.D. *Understanding Your Child's Temperament.* New York: Macmillan, 1997. Helps parents gain insight into a child's nine inborn temperamental traits and suggests ways to make "a better fit" between these normal traits and the child's environment; useful from infancy through adolescence.

Caron, Ann F., Ed.D. *Don't Stop Loving Me: A Reassuring Guide for Mothers of Adolescent Daughters.* New York: Harper Perennial, 1991. Describes how the mother-daughter relationship changes during adolescence and deals with the presence or absence of Dad.

Drill, Esther, Heather McDonald and Rebecca Odes. *Deal with It!* New York: Pocket Books, 1999. An appealing presentation targeted at adolescent girls; full of information about their bodies, brains, and life in general.

Drinkmeyer, Don, and Gary McKay. *Parenting Teenagers.* Circle Pines, MN: American Guidance Service, 1990. A workbook of exercises addressing encouragement, communication, and discipline; explains teens' motivations and their reactions to parents.

Gabriel, H. Paul, M.D., and Robert Wool. *Anticipating Adolescence.* New York: Henry Holt and Company, 1995. Addresses specific problems (such as eating disorders, substance abuse, and divorce) as well as ways to cope with a teen's emotional upheaval and forge better relationships.

Garbarino, Dr. James. *Lost Boys: Why Our Sons Turn Violent and How We Can Save Them.* New York: Free Press, 1999. A study of why boys turn violent and ways to identify and help those who may become violent.

Giannetti, Charlene C., and Margaret Sagarese. *The Roller-Coaster Years*. New York: Broadway Books, 1997. How to enjoy and survive what the authors call the "maddening yet magical middle school years."

Goldstein, Robin. *"Stop Treating Me Like a Kid!" Everyday Parenting: The 10- to 13-Year-Old*. New York: Penguin Books, 1994. Ways to talk and listen to teens, their opinions of family members, physical changes, self-image, independence, responsibility, peer influence, school behavior, drugs, and everyday conflicts.

Gottman, John, Ph.D. with Joan DeClaire. *The Heart of Parenting: Raising an Emotionally Intelligent Child*. New York: Simon & Schuster, 1997. Shows parents how to become "emotion coaches" to help children master feelings such as anxiety and impulsivity so that they can become more self-confident and handle emotional crises.

Gurian, Michael. *The Good Son: Shaping the Moral Development of Our Boys and Young Men*. New York: Putnam, 1999. A therapist's study of moral and emotional development; by author of *The Wonder of Boys*.

Johnson, Eric W. *People, Love, Sex, and Families: Answers to Questions That Preteens Ask*. New York: Walker and Co., 1985. Like the same author's *Love and Sex in Plain Language* (Bantam Books, 1988), this offers a straightforward and clear approach to a subject that many parents find awkward.

Madaras, Lynda, with Dane Saavedra. *What's Happening to My Body? Book for Boys*. New York: Newmarket Press, 1987. A mother-son collaboration that clearly explains physical, emotional, and lifestyle changes as boys approach puberty.

Madaras, Lynda, with Area Madaras. *What's Happening to My Body? Book for Girls.* New York: Newmarket Press, 1987. The mother-daughter version of the preceding title.

McCoy, Kathy, and Charles Wibbelsman. *Growing and Changing: A Handbook for Preteens.* New York: Putnam, 1987. Useful for teens to read themselves.

Nelsen, Jane, and Lynn Lott. *Positive Discipline for Teenagers: Resolving Conflict with Your Teenage Son or Daughter.* Rocklin, CA: Prima Publishing, 1994. Explores skills to win cooperation from your teen, understand rebellion, balance control and punishment, and grow with your teenager.

Panzarine, Susan. *A Parent's Guide to the Teen Years: Raising Your 11- to 14-Year-Old in the Age of Chat Rooms and Navel Rings.* New York: Facts on File, Inc., Checkmark Books, 2000. A lively guide to physical, emotional, and cognitive changes to expect during these transition years.

Pollack, William S., Ph.D. *Real Boys: Rescuing Our Sons from the Myths of Boyhood.* New York: Henry Holt, 1999. Explains how conventional notions about masculinity do boys a disservice; how they struggle with mixed messages and conflicting expectations.

Ponton, Lynn E. *The Romance of Risk: Why Teenagers Do What They Do.* New York: Basic Books, 1998. While most risk-taking is normal in adolescence, this book looks at fifteen case studies of troubled teens' harmful risk-taking; suggests ways to redirect it into safer directions.

Rushford, Patricia H. *Have You Hugged Your Teenager Today? A Six-Point Strategy for Maximizing Love and Minimizing Guilt.* Grand Rapids, MI: Fleming H. Revell, 1983. Explores reasons why some parents feel guilty toward their teens; discusses how to hug your teen; and how to let go.

Slap, Gail B., M.D., and Martha M. Jablow. *Teenage Health Care.* New York: Pocket Books, 1994. A comprehensive guide to the physical, psychological, and behavioral issues that affect an adolescent's well-being; called "the Dr. Spock for teenagers."

Swets, Paul W. *The Art of Talking with Your Teenager.* Holbrook, MA: Adams Publishing, 1995. Helps parents listen and hear what teens are really saying; gives advice for interpreting their messages and staying calm in tough situations.

Tracy, Louise Felton, M.S. *Grounded for Life?! Stop Blowing Your Fuse and Start Communicating with Your Teenager.* Seattle: Parenting Press, Inc., 1994. A humorous book that shows parents how to relax and see adolescence in the bigger picture; ways to change confrontation to calm communication.

Wolf, Anthony E., Ph.D. *Get Out of My Life, But First Could You Drive Me and Cheryl to the Mall?* New York: Harper-Collins, 1991. This popular, witty guide clarifies why adolescents do and say the things they do and helps guide parents toward living with them in a more compassionate way.

Other Resources

AIDS Hot Line: 800-342-AIDS. Information and educational services, medical and support group referrals; sponsored by the Centers for Disease Control and Prevention.

Alcohol and Drug Abuse Helpline: 800-252-6465.

American Anorexia/Bulimia Association: 212-501-8351. Information on eating disorders; referrals and outreach programs.

Daughters, a newsletter for parents of girls ages 10 to 16, available by subscription: 1-888-849-8476 or through its website: www.daughters@americangirl.com.

Child Abuse Hot Line: 800-422-4453. 24-hour counseling service.

Children with Attention Deficit Disorders (CHADD): 1-305-587-3700.

Mothers Against Drunk Driving (MADD): 1-800-GET-MADD. Website: www.madd.org P.O. Box 541688, Dallas, TX 75354-1688.

National Institute on Drug Abuse: 301-443-6245. Referrals for drug-abuse prevention programs.

National Youth Violence Prevention Center: www.safe youth.org.

Parents, Families, and Friends of Lesbians and Gays, Inc.: 1-800-4-FAMILY.

Runaway Hot Line: 800-231-6946. Accepts phone calls from runaways; offers free bus ride home, forwards messages to home, and provides referrals for medical aid and shelter.

Sexually Transmitted Diseases Hot Line: 800-227-8922.

Students Against Destructive Decisions (SADD): 877-SADD-INC (toll-free). SADD, Inc. (also known as Students Against Driving Drunk). Website: www.saddonline .com or SADD National, Box 800, Marlboro, MA 01752.

Index